PRAISE FOR DATA–MINDED

"Data is the lifeblood of the digital economy, and data-oriented businesses require a unique mindset and toolkit for success. Seasoned entrepreneurs Jonathan Chin and Lorn Davis provide an essential roadmap for this exciting new ecosystem. A must-read for entrepreneurs, business students and academics, and practitioners hoping to learn about DaaS."

- Jialan Wang, Associate Professor of Finance at University of Illinois & NBER Research Associate

"As alternative data moves from unfamiliar to essential, there is nobody better than Jonathan Chin & Lorn Davis to share with us the historical context of how we got here & ponder with us the future of data. Data-Minded is a must read for anyone working in the business of data."

- John Farrall, Creator of The Alt Data Weekly

DATA-MINDED

DATA-MINDED

An Entrepreneur's Guide
to a Data Startup

Jonathan Chin
Lorn Davis

Foreword by Douglas B. Laney

Øin
ZERO IN PRESS
Oregon

Published in the United States by Zero In Press.
www.0in.io

Library of Congress Cataloging-in-Publication Data is on file with the publisher.

ISBN Harcover: 979-8-9906239-0-3
ISBN eBook: 979-8-9906239-1-0

Printed in the United States of America

Cover designed by William Loccisano
Book designed by Jonathan Chin

*To our beloved families, whose love and support
have been the foundation of our journey. Your belief
in us and our dreams has given us the courage
to explore uncharted entrepreneurial territories,
moving among dragons to uncover (data) gold.*

CONTENTS

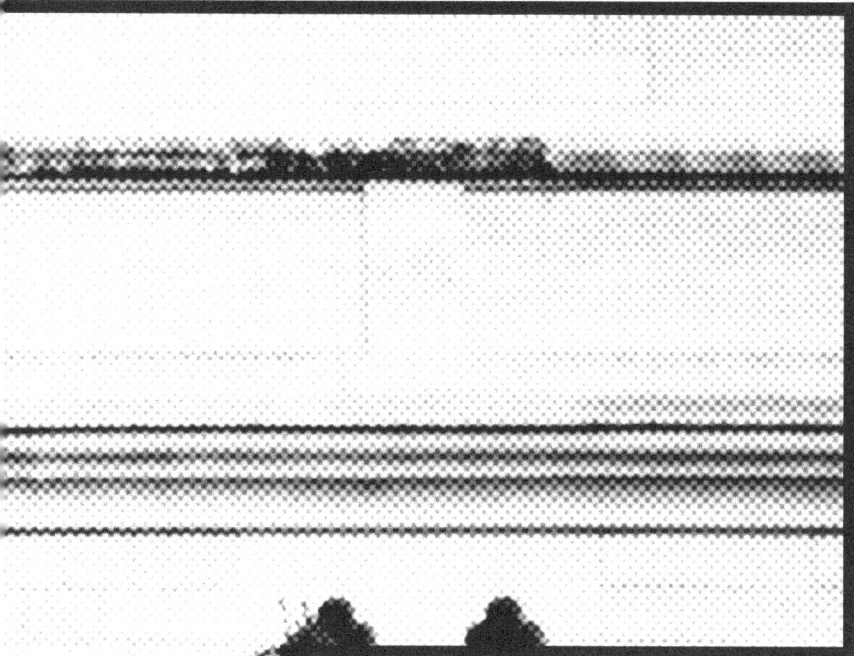

FOREWORD

FOREWORD

In today's and especially tomorrow's business worlds in which data is no longer a byproduct but rather a core and increasingly recognized business asset, "Data-Minded: An Entrepreneur's Guide to a Data Startup" by Jonathan Chin and Lorn Davis serves as a much-needed compass. This book is more than just a guide; it is a revelation and a manifesto that encourages entrepreneurs to embrace the data era with open minds and open wallets.

The book's themes are strikingly relevant and deeply resonant, advancing the concept of infonomics, the doctrine I developed over a decade ago that champions monetizing, managing, and measuring data as an enterprise asset.

Data has transformed from an underutilized asset into the lifeblood of innovation and strategic decision-making. "Data-Minded" expertly navigates this paradigm shift, providing readers with a comprehensive understanding of how to capitalize on data's inherent value. The book's examination of data productization is a prime example of the infonomics principle of data monetization. It meticulously demonstrates how raw data can be transformed into marketable and valuable products, a process that is essential for any data-driven entrepreneurial venture.

Their journey, however, does not begin and end with data productization. The management of data, a principle central to infonomics, is another cornerstone of this book. Chin and Davis delve into the nuances of managing data as a strategic asset, providing insights into the complex dynamics of data governance, quality control, and privacy considerations. Their discussion on these topics is not only theoretical; it is also grounded in practical wisdom and real-world application, making it an invaluable resource for entrepreneurs.

The book also addresses the critical issue of determining the economic value of data. Understanding the financial implications of data is critical in an age when data is considered an asset. This is consistent with the infonomics tenet of quantifying data's economic impact. The authors' approach to this topic is both insightful and pragmatic, giving readers the tools they need to calculate the financial benefits of their data initiatives.

"Data-Minded" also stands out in its treatment of marketing and sales strategies tailored to data products. In a market flooded with conventional strategies and a fixation on low-value dashboards and the like, this book provides a fresh perspective on how to define, market, and sell data products effectively. This demonstrates the authors' extensive knowledge of the data industry's unique challenges and opportunities and the growing appetite for data, particularly in light of recent advances in AI.

Furthermore, the book's foray into the ethical dimensions of data handling is both timely and necessary. In a world increasingly concerned with data privacy and ethical use, Chin and Davis prompt readers to consider the broader societal implications of their data practices. This aspect of the book is especially powerful because it instills in data entrepreneurs a sense of responsibility and societal stewardship.

"Data-Minded" is more than just a book; it is a beacon for the future of data entrepreneurship. This book serves as a vital guide as we navigate the complexities of a data-driven world, illuminating the path for entrepreneurs who want to harness the power of data. Chin and Davis' insights are not just theoretical musings; they are practical, actionable, and grounded in real-world experiences.

"Data-Minded" is a seminal work in the emerging field of infonomics, serving as an indispensable resource for anyone aspiring to success in the data industry. This book is more than just informative; it further inspires a new way of thinking about data as an invaluable asset that, when administered and deployed with discipline, can unlock innovative and incredible business benefits.

Douglas B. Laney

Innovation Fellow, Data & Analytics
Strategy, West Monroe

Author of
Infonomics: How to Monetize, Manage,
and Measure Information as an Asset for
Competitive Advantage, and

Data Juice: 101 Real-World Stories of
How Organizations Are Squeezing Value
From Available Data Assets

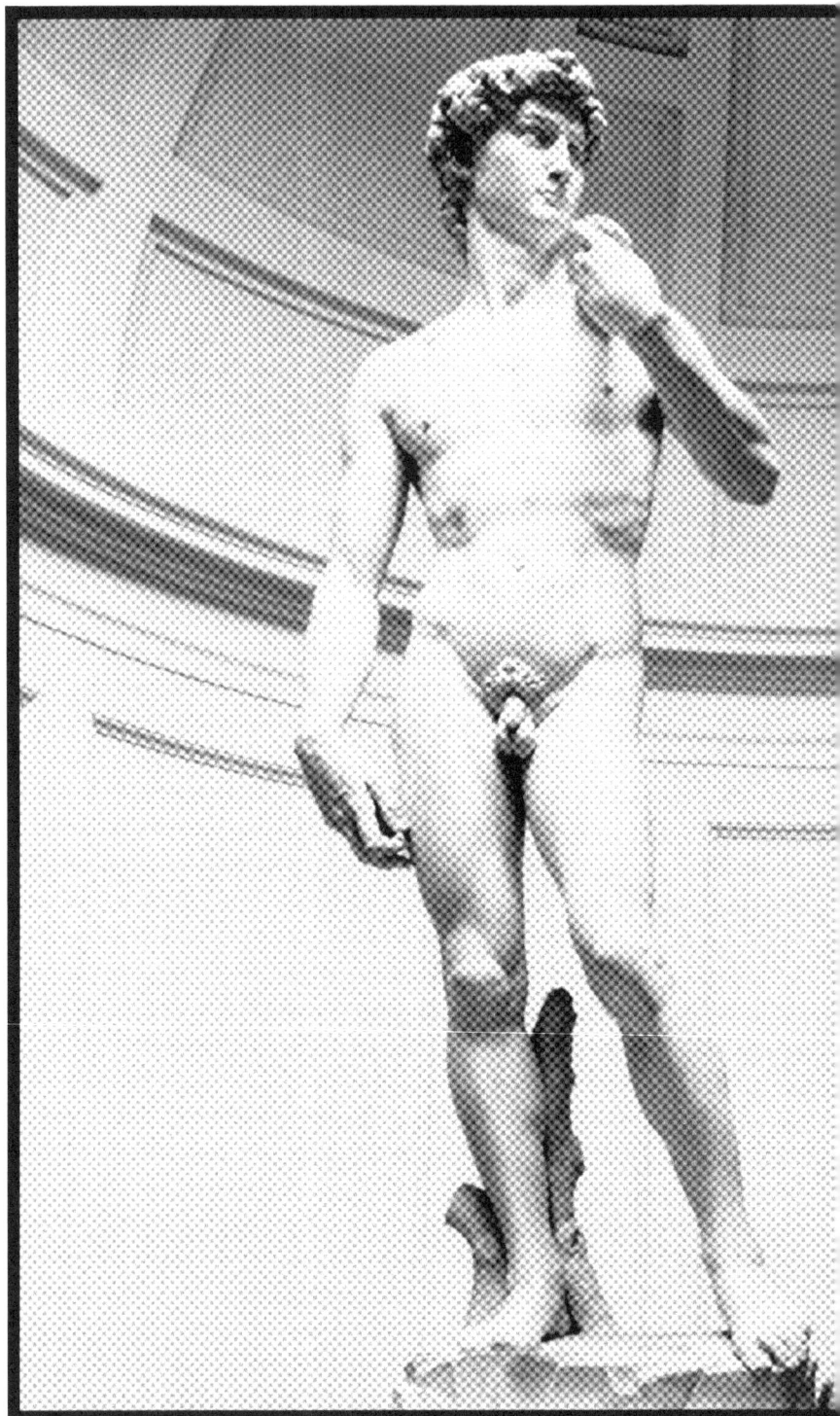

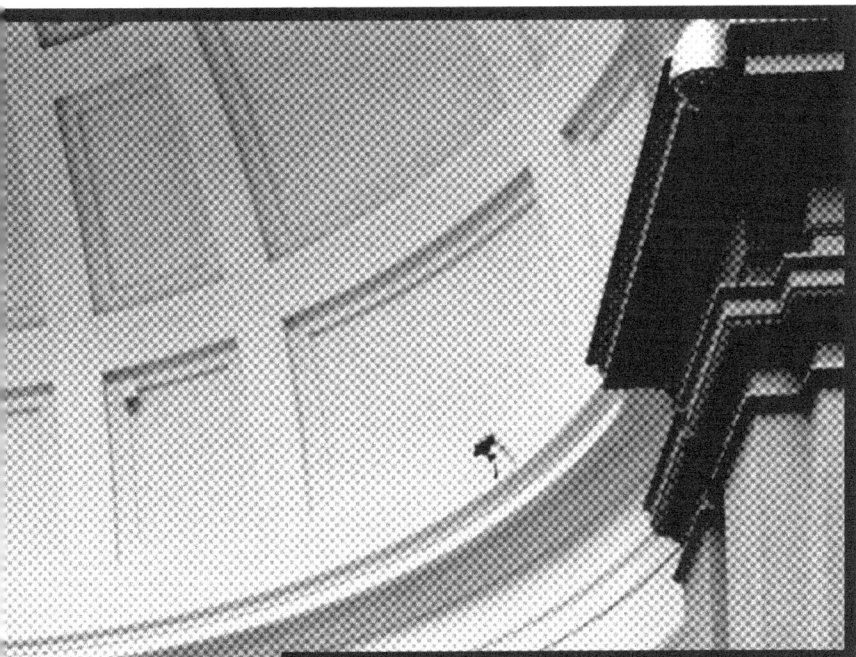

INTRODUCTION

INTRODUCTION

The modern world runs on data. Whether it's user data, geolocation data, transaction data, financial data, or environmental data, today's businesses are directed by the ways they collect, consume, and analyze data. Yet despite the growing prevalence of big data in the digital era, there are still many misconceptions about what exactly a data company is.

Often confused with software companies and apps, data companies are distinct entities that specialize in collecting, analyzing, and interpreting information to help businesses like yours make informed decisions. Unlike software companies that primarily focus on developing and selling software products, data companies leverage advanced analytics to tap into the potential of data. This enables them to reveal concealed insights and emerging patterns, empowering their teams and clients to optimize strategies, streamline operations, and achieve unprecedented growth. The best data companies are experts at turning raw information into actionable intelligence.

Our mission in this book is to break down how data companies are shaping today's marketplace. We offer a comprehensive exploration of the history of data, the pulse of the modern data industry, and indispensable strategies for launching, expanding, positioning, and steering a thriving data enterprise.

Plus, we've got all the must-know tips for managing the ins and outs of a successful data business. Forget old-school thinking. Data companies don't stick to rigid code. The role data plays in your customers' businesses is not static the way it might be with software. Instead, the data business is all about managing and shaping the data into a usable form within set parameters. This means data businesses themselves are also constantly changing—adapting to the unpredictable nature of data until it reaches a critical moment of growth.

The journey of starting a data company is not for the faint-hearted. It's a thrilling adventure where you're not just managing data, but also shaping it into something valuable and organized amidst the chaos.

In Chapter 1, we explore the rich histories of data companies and how they have evolved over time, showing how important data has always been. Understanding the history of data companies is essential for navigating the complexities of the current modern digital landscape. By tracing their evolution, we gain valuable context and insight into the origins of key practices, technologies, and challenges. We'll look at the paths of early pioneers who set the stage for today's data-driven industries.

Chapter 2 introduces the concept of 'data productization,' a crucial process for succeeding in today's market. In simple terms, it's about transforming raw data into valuable insights that can be packaged and sold to businesses. We'll explore how to craft data products that grab people's attention by offering actionable solutions, compelling visualizations, and personalized insights tailored to specific needs and interests. This chapter debunks misconceptions about product development in data companies, emphasizing that they are more like miners and refiners extracting value from raw data through collection, curation, and enhancement rather than architects and builders constructing products from the ground up. By the end, we'll better understand the unique dynamics of data product development and how to unlock the true potential of data.

In Chapter 3, we discuss marketing in the world of data companies. We'll uncover the power of subtle influence and strategic networking, where deeper connections, trust-building, and the exchange of valuable insights matter more than big announcements and flashy campaigns. When it comes to sales, think less used-car pitch and more matchmaker, connecting singular data products with their soulmate applications. In this chapter, we address misconceptions about marketing strategies for data companies, highlighting that, unlike software companies with straightforward, problem-solving value propositions, data companies must navigate a more nuanced approach. By the end, we'll grasp the importance of showcasing the versatility and adaptability of data products while inspiring customers to envision the vast possibilities for their unique needs, mastering the art of marketing the potential and promise of data.

In Chapter 4, we'll explore the 'art of data sales,' a unique approach where we shift from showcasing features to crafting a compelling narrative around the untapped potential within the data. We'll learn the delicate balance of creating the perfect data sample and aligning it with customer needs while safeguarding intellectual property. This chapter also debunks misconceptions, emphasizing the importance of transparency and ethics in data representation. By the end, we'll be well-equipped to navigate the unique dynamics of data sales and unlock the true potential of our data.

Finally, Chapter 5 looks at the world of crafting a compelling business case and the 'murky waters of financing,' where bold ventures chase after valuable data. It's a risky game, as investing in data can involve substantial upfront costs, as well as uncertainties regarding data quality and relevance. Moreover, the data landscape is constantly evolving, making it challenging to accurately predict future market trends and demands. However, for those who dare to take the plunge, the rewards can be significant, ranging from gaining a competitive edge to unlocking new revenue streams and innovative business opportunities. This chapter also clarifies misconceptions about financing and fundraising for data companies, emphasizing that, unlike software companies with a linear value creation process, data companies require significant upfront investment to reach a 'critical mass' of high-quality, relevant data before delivering value. By the end, we'll understand the importance of patience, a long-term vision, and a compelling narrative when fundraising for data companies, given the unique dynamics of their value-creation process.

This book is not just a collection of facts and strategies. It's a journey, a story of triumphs and follies, drawn from our decades of collective experience in the data industry. We started with nothing more than an idea—that consumer spending data could be transformative when understood and leveraged correctly—and built our company from scratch. As entrepreneurs with a combined 30 years in the data industry, we understand that data is more than a resource—it's a complex terrain demanding adept navigation. Our journey includes pivotal breakthroughs, like pioneering a new category of consumer spending insights for retailers and restaurants using at-scale real-time debit and credit card transactions, disrupting reliance on small samples, slow surveys, and other methods, which reshaped industry paradigms and established us as leaders. Throughout our years of experience, our unwavering commitment to excellence and our passion for data empowerment have been our guiding forces.

Bringing insights from our entrepreneurial journey, we'll provide you with the tools and strategies essential for navigating the dynamic data industry. Whether you're a seasoned pro or new to the field, our roadmap offers actionable advice, compelling narratives, and invaluable insights to illuminate your way forward. If you're ready to embark on a journey of discovery and transformation, come along as we explore the boundless realms of possibility and opportunity in the modern data landscape.

CHAPTER 1
THE DAWN OF DATA

THE DAWN OF DATA

Before we begin discussing what makes modern data companies unique, it is important to explore the genesis of data over the past several thousand years. We're currently at a critical juncture one might call The Dawn of The Data Company. The differences between present-day data companies and their predecessors can be mainly attributed to technological advancements and the digitization of nearly everything. Still, the systems and assumptions inherent in modern data companies have roots spreading all the way back to 4000 B.C. From the earliest forms of record-keeping and census-taking to the development of complex statistical methods and data-processing techniques, the history of data is a long and fascinating one. Understanding this history is essential for appreciating the significance of the current moment and the unique challenges and opportunities facing modern data companies.

Over the past couple hundred years, data companies have emerged as pioneers in collecting, organizing, and analyzing information. Their primary purpose has been to support businesses and governments in making informed decisions based on facts and figures. These companies often focused on specific uses, such as finance, market research, or banking, and relied heavily on manual processes and rudimentary technology. The early data companies laid the foundation for the modern data industry by establishing the basic principles and practices of data collection, analysis, and dissemination. However, their ability to handle large volumes of data and perform complex analyses was limited by the technology of the time.

As the digital revolution unfolded, the data industry began to evolve in parallel with technological advancement, namely the creation of microchips. The advent of computers and the internet transformed the way data was created, collected, stored, and processed. This paved the way for the development of more sophisticated data systems and tools, enabling data companies to unlock and access vast amounts of information that were once too unwieldy to analyze or even collect. The digital revolution also gave rise to entirely new types of data, such as social media data, sensor data, geolocation data, and clickstream data, which opened up new possibilities for data-driven insights and decision-making. This explosion of data and the tools to analyze it marked a turning point in the evolution of data companies.

Today's data companies have transcended their traditional ancillary roles, becoming vital components in the modern business landscape. They are no longer simply providers of single-threaded facts or basic analytics; they are now partners that enable organizations to derive strategic value from data. With the proliferation of big data, artificial intelligence (AI), and machine learning, data companies have gained the ability to harness unprecedented levels of information, turning them into actionable insights that can drive business growth, innovation, and competitive advantage. The rise of cloud computing and the democratization of data tools have also made it easier for smaller companies and startups to enter the data industry, leading to increased competition and innovation. As a result, modern data companies are at the forefront of some of the most exciting and transformative developments in business and society today.

What is a modern data company?

A data company is an organization that leverages access to data as its core asset to create value for its customers and stakeholders. This value can be delivered in many forms, such as providing access to unique data sets, developing advanced analytics solutions, or offering AI-powered tools enabling users to make data-driven decisions. Data companies often specialize in specific domains or industries, such as finance, healthcare, or marketing, and tailor their data offerings to meet the unique needs of their target customers. They may also differentiate themselves through their data collection and processing capabilities, proprietary algorithms, or the insights they can generate from their data assets. Ultimately, the success of a data company hinges on its ability to transform raw data into actionable intelligence that drives business value for its clients.

Modern data companies are concerned not only with the technical aspects of data management and analysis but also with the ethical use of data, ensuring that privacy, security, continuity, and fairness are maintained throughout the entire lifecycle. This focus on responsible data practices is essential in building customer trust and fostering a sustainable and equitable data business. Data companies must navigate complex regulatory landscapes like GLBA, GDPR, PCI, and CCPA while adhering to industry-specific standards and best practices. They must implement robust data governance frameworks, secure data storage and transmission protocols, and transparent data handling processes.

In today's world, a data company is an organization that sits at the intersection of technology, domain expertise, and unique or proprietary access. As we witness the rapid evolution of the data landscape, data companies will play an increasingly pivotal role in shaping the future of business, technology, and society. Data companies will also be at the forefront of developing new technologies, such as advanced artificial intelligence and machine learning algorithms, like generative ai, that will transform how we live and work. As data becomes an increasingly critical asset for organizations of all sizes and industries, the importance of data companies will only continue to grow, positioning them as key players in the digital economy of the future.

A Brief History of Data and Data Companies

In the modern era, data has emerged as one of the most valuable resources, driving innovation, decision-making, and economic growth across nearly every industry. The ability to collect, process, and analyze vast amounts of information has become a key competitive advantage for businesses, governments, and organizations of all kinds.

From the ingenious attempts at collecting and recording information in ancient civilizations to the cutting-edge AI-driven data companies of the 21st century, the history of data and data companies is a testament to human ingenuity and technological progress. We will investigate the milestones, innovations, and turning points that have shaped the current data revolution, highlighting the role of visionary thinkers and their groundbreaking inventions. From the earliest forms of writing and record-keeping to the development of statistical methods and computing technologies, we will trace the evolution of data and data companies over the centuries. Along the way, we will encounter individuals who have paved the way for the data-driven world we live in today, leaving you in awe of their foresight and innovation.

By understanding the origins of data companies and the factors contributing to their evolution, we can better appreciate their significance in today's world and anticipate future trends and challenges. Through this journey, we will gain valuable insights into the opportunities associated with the data revolution and the role that data companies will play in shaping the future of business, society, and the world at large.

THE EARLY DAYS: STATISTICS AND CENSUS DATA

We can trace the roots of data collection and analysis back to ancient civilizations, where rudimentary forms of data management were utilized for various administrative purposes. The ancient Babylonians, for example, recorded their census data on clay tablets around 4000 B.C., with detailed information about agriculture, commerce, and population. This early data collection enabled them to plan and allocate resources more effectively, ensuring the prosperity and stability of their society. The Babylonians' meticulous record-keeping laid the foundation for future civilizations to build upon, and their data collection and storage methods were remarkably advanced for their time. The use of clay tablets allowed for the preservation of these records for thousands of years, providing invaluable insights into the lives and practices of ancient peoples.

Similarly, the ancient Incas of South America stand out for their unique and sophisticated system, known as the Quipu. The Quipu was an intricate arrangement of knotted cords used by the Incas to record and communicate a wide array of information vital to the administration of their expansive empire. Unlike the written scripts of contemporary civilizations, the Incas' Quipu employed a visual and tactile method for data representation, where the color, length, and arrangement of knots on variously colored strings encoded details about population, agricultural yields, and even historical events. The Quipu system was highly efficient and accurate, allowing the Incas to manage their vast empire effectively. Despite the lack of a written language, the Incas were able to maintain a complex and organized society through their innovative use of data management techniques.

The Egyptians also maintained extensive taxation and resource management records, as seen in their preserved papyrus scrolls. By keeping track of their agricultural output, workforce, and taxation data, the Egyptians could optimize their economy and support large-scale projects, such as the construction of the Great Pyramids. The Egyptians' use of papyrus as a writing material was a significant advancement in data storage, as it allowed for more detailed and extensive record-keeping than clay tablets or stone inscriptions. The survival of many of these papyrus scrolls to the present day has provided historians with a wealth of information about ancient Egyptian society and its advanced data management systems.

The Roman Empire was not the first nor the last to run periodic censuses, but they certainly applied it at a massive scale. The practice continued for centuries, providing valuable insights into the empire's demographics, economy, and infrastructure. This information was used to effectively administer Rome's vast territories, maintain public infrastructure, and supply its formidable military forces. The Romans' extensive use of census data was a critical factor in their ability to maintain control over their empire for centuries. By regularly collecting and analyzing data on their population and resources, the Romans were able to make informed decisions about taxation, public works projects, and military campaigns.

One of the most renowned early records is the Domesday Book, commissioned by William the Conqueror in 1086 AD, which meticulously documented land ownership, resources, and population numbers in England. This comprehensive survey allowed the Norman king to assess the wealth and resources of his newly acquired kingdom, facilitating efficient taxation and resource allocation. The Domesday Book is considered one of the most remarkable administrative records of the Middle Ages, and its creation marked a significant milestone in the history of data collection and analysis. The level of detail and organization in the Domesday Book was unprecedented for its time and served as a model for future surveys and censuses.

These early instances of data collection set the stage for more advanced forms of data analysis that would emerge centuries later. The use of data has been a driving force behind the rise and fall of empires, the development of new technologies and industries, and the shaping of human society as a whole. By examining the impact of data on these ancient societies, we can better appreciate its transformative power and the crucial role it will continue to play in modern times.

THE INDUSTRIAL REVOLUTION: BIRTH OF MODERN DATA ANALYSIS

The Industrial Revolution in the 18th and 19th centuries witnessed a significant turning point in the history of data. Rapid industrialization, urbanization, and burgeoning global trade networks generated an unprecedented amount of information. This information boom led to the development of more sophisticated data analysis techniques to make sense of the complex data landscape. The need for efficient data management and analysis became increasingly apparent as businesses and governments sought to optimize their operations and gain a competitive edge. This period marked the beginning of a new era in which data would play an increasingly central role in shaping the course of human history.

Pioneering statisticians such as John Graunt and William Playfair played pivotal roles in shaping the early field of data science. In the mid-17th century, Graunt analyzed London's Bills of Mortality, which documented the city's weekly births, deaths, and causes of death. By scrutinizing these records, he uncovered ways in population growth, life expectancy, and disease prevalence. His insights revolutionized the field of demography and provided valuable information to city planners, helping to improve public health policies and mitigate the impact of epidemics. Graunt's work laid the foundation for the development of modern epidemiology and demonstrated the power of data analysis in understanding complex social phenomena.

In the late 18th century, Scottish engineer and political economist William Playfair revolutionized modern graphical representations of data, such as bar charts, line graphs, and pie charts. These innovations dramatically transformed the speed at which people understood and communicated complex data, which enabled businesses, governments, and scientists to make more informed decisions and develop data-driven policies. Playfair's work was particularly influential in the fields of economics and social science, where his charts and graphs helped illuminate patterns and trends that had previously been hidden in raw data. His contributions to the field of data visualization continue to be celebrated and built upon by data scientists and designers to this day.

Playfair's groundbreaking data visualization techniques remain relevant today as they continue to shape how we understand and interpret complex data. His charts have become essential tools for representing statistical information in a clear and accessible manner. The principles of clarity, simplicity, and visual appeal that Playfair pioneered continue to guide the development of new data visualization techniques and tools.

More recent innovations based on Playfair's work, such as interactive visualizations, infographics, and even immersive virtual reality experiences, now enable more effective communication of data-driven insights than ever before. These new technologies have opened up new possibilities for engaging audiences and conveying complex information in a way that is both informative and entertaining. As data becomes increasingly central to our lives and work, the importance of effective data visualization and communication will only continue to grow. The legacy of William Playfair and other early pioneers in the field of data science will continue to inspire and guide us as we navigate this new landscape.

During this same era, Florence Nightingale, a celebrated nurse and statistician, utilized data visualization techniques to demonstrate the correlation between poor sanitation and high mortality rates in British military hospitals during the Crimean War. Nightingale meticulously collected and analyzed data on the conditions of the hospitals, ultimately presenting her findings in the form of a 'rose diagram,' which powerfully illustrated the devastating impact of unsanitary conditions on soldiers' health. Her work was groundbreaking not only for its use of data analysis and visualization but also for its focus on the social determinants of health. Nightingale's insights into the importance of sanitation and hygiene in preventing disease and promoting health continue to influence public health policies and practices to this day.

Nightingale's innovative use of data analysis and visualization led to significant improvements in healthcare standards, both in military and civilian settings. By implementing her recommendations, the British government was able to drastically reduce mortality rates and improve the overall well-being of its military personnel. Her pioneering work in nursing and public health, fueled by her passion for data, left a legacy that continues to inspire healthcare professionals and data scientists today. Her contributions to the field of healthcare and data science cannot be overstated, and her legacy continues to shape our understanding of the power of data to drive social change and improve lives.

Around this time, collecting, analyzing, and communicating institutional data became a fundamental aspect of any organization. The rise of bureaucracy and the growth of large-scale enterprises created a need for more sophisticated data management and analysis techniques. Governments, businesses, and other institutions began to invest in the development of new technologies and methods for collecting, storing, and analyzing data.

THE INFORMATION AGE: THE ADVENT OF COMPUTERS AND THE INTERNET

The 20th century heralded the Information Age, catalyzed by the rise of computers and the internet, which laid the groundwork for the modern data companies this book focuses on. As we explore this period, we'll uncover the connections between the development of technology and the increased generation, analysis, and utilization of data. The exponential growth of data during this era was not just a byproduct of technological advancement but a driving force behind it, as the need to process and make sense of vast amounts of information spurred the development of more powerful computing tools and techniques.

The transition from analog to digital data storage methods marked a pivotal shift in the scale and scope of data handling. This evolution enabled an unprecedented expansion in data accessibility and manipulation, unshackled by the constraints of physical space and the labor-intensive processes associated with traditional methods. It was not merely a technological advancement but a fundamental change in how we perceive and interact with data. The digitization of data made it possible to store, process, and analyze vast amounts of information in ways that were previously unimaginable, opening up new frontiers in fields and disciplines ranging from science and medicine to business and government.

In 1936, an English mathematician and computer scientist, Alan Turing, conceptualized the Turing Machine, laying the foundation for the first programmable computer. In 1946, the Electronic Numerical Integrator and Computer (ENIAC) was born, capable of solving complex mathematical problems. This breakthrough ignited the development of various computing machines, such as the UNIVAC I (1951), the first commercially available computer, and the IBM System/360 (1964), a pioneering mainframe computer that transformed data processing. These early computers allowed businesses and governments to process and analyze vast amounts of information more efficiently, enabling them to make informed decisions and optimize their operations. The development of these machines marked a turning point in the history of computing, as they demonstrated the potential of automated data processing to transform every aspect of human society. The impact of these early computers can still be felt today, as they laid the groundwork for the development of the powerful computing tools and platforms that drive the modern data economy.

The launch of ARPANET in 1969, the precursor to the modern internet, marked a significant milestone in the evolution of data sharing and communication. In 1989, Tim Berners-Lee invented the World Wide Web, further revolutionizing the way data was collected, stored, and shared. This accessibility made vast amounts of information available to people globally, facilitating the growth of digital data. The ability to access and share data on a global scale opened up new opportunities for collaboration, innovation, and economic growth, laying the foundation for the emergence of new industries and business models based on the power of data.

Moving into the 21st century, we saw the rise of personal computers, search engines, and social media platforms propelling the growth of digital data, creating an abundance of information that could be leveraged for various purposes. Businesses began to use data to gain insights into customer preferences, optimize marketing strategies, and make data-driven decisions. Governments utilized data for better policymaking, public service delivery, and tracking social trends. The growing importance of data sets the stage for the Big Data era and the emergence of data companies that would harness the power of information to drive innovation and economic growth. As we continue to generate and collect ever-increasing amounts of data, the need for effective data management, analysis, and governance has become more pressing than ever before. The emergence of data companies specializing in these areas is a natural response to this need, as organizations seek to leverage the power of data to drive innovation and insight, improve decision-making, and gain a competitive edge in an increasingly data-driven world.

THE EMERGENCE OF MODERN DATA COMPANIES

As the volume and variety of data increased, it created fertile ground for specialized data companies to serve existing purposes more efficiently and novel purposes previously unimaginable. These companies, with their focus on collecting, processing, and distributing data, have not only met the growing demand for actionable insights but have also transformed industries. The emergence of these specialized data companies was a natural response to the increasing complexity and scale of data being generated and the growing recognition of the value that data-driven insights could provide to businesses and organizations. As data became increasingly recognized as a valuable asset, the demand for specialized data services and solutions proliferated, driving innovation and competition in the data industry.

The foundation of modern data companies can be traced back to the early 20th century, with pioneers like the Nielsen Company playing a key role in shaping the industry. Founded in the 1920s by Arthur C. Nielsen, Sr., the Nielsen Company began as a marketing research firm, initially employing methods akin to those used in the Census, focusing on direct data collection from individuals. This approach was revolutionary for its time, providing businesses with insight into consumer behavior and product popularity. As technology evolved, so did Nielsen's methods. The company seamlessly transitioned from manual data collection to harnessing electronic sales and inventory systems, reflecting a broader industry trend toward automated data gathering. This shift increased the efficiency and scope of data collection and marked a significant transformation in how data was used to understand and influence consumer behavior. Nielsen's journey from manual surveys to sophisticated electronic data analysis charts the evolution of the data industry, highlighting a path from direct, labor-intensive methods to the seamless integration of technology in data acquisition and analysis. The Nielsen Company's evolution is a testament to the adaptability and innovation that has characterized the data industry from its earliest days, setting the stage for the rapid growth and transformation that would follow in the decades to come.

In the 1960s, Quotron Systems Inc. provided the first electronic stock market quotations to financial professionals, paving the way for what became known as alternative (non-primary sourced) data companies. These companies later leveraged vast amounts of non-traditional data sources to generate unique insights into market trends and investment opportunities, giving their clients a competitive edge.

In the 1970s and 1980s, companies like LexisNexis and Bloomberg emerged, offering comprehensive databases of legal, financial, and news information. These data companies revolutionized how professionals accessed and utilized data in their respective fields, streamlining research processes and enabling more informed decision-making. The success of these early data companies demonstrated the immense value of curated, specialized data sets. The ability to quickly and easily access relevant information was a game-changer for professionals across a wide range of industries, from law and finance to journalism and academia. The emergence of these specialized data providers was foundational for the development of the modern data industry as more and more companies began to recognize the value of data as a strategic asset.

The introduction of Geographic Information Systems (GIS) in the 1980s further expanded the data landscape, enabling the analysis and visualization of spatial data. This technology facilitated the development of location-based services and geospatial analytics, creating new opportunities for data companies to offer innovative solutions across various industries, such as urban planning, disaster management, and environmental monitoring. The ability to integrate and analyze spatial data with other types of data, such as demographic, economic, and environmental data, opened up new possibilities for understanding and addressing complex challenges in a wide range of fields. The development of GIS technology also paved the way for the emergence of new types of data companies specializing in location-based services and geospatial analytics, further diversifying the data industry.

As the Information Age progressed, the increasing generation and availability of data drove the need for advanced data processing and analytics tools. This demand led to the development of sophisticated software solutions for data mining, predictive analytics, and machine learning, which would become essential components of modern data companies. The ability to process and analyze vast amounts of data quickly and accurately became a key differentiator for data companies as businesses and organizations increasingly sought to leverage data-driven insights. The development of these advanced data analytics tools also opened up new opportunities for data companies to offer specialized services and solutions, such as predictive maintenance, fraud detection, customer segmentation, targeting marketing, and forecasting, further expanding the scope and impact of the data industry.

In the next section, we will take a closer look at influential data companies that represent prime examples of how data companies were created and how they evolved.

These insights will enable us to look to the future of data companies and how we might stay ahead of the curve as part of a long line of data pioneers. By understanding the key drivers and trends that have shaped the development of the data industry over time, we can gain valuable insights into the challenges and opportunities that lie ahead and position ourselves to capitalize on the ongoing data revolution.

THE CREDIT BUREAUS: A DATA-DRIVEN APPROACH TO FINANCIAL HISTORY

Throughout human history, trade has been a cornerstone of growing civilizations, fostering economic development and cultural exchange. Central to the expansion of trade was the concept of credit, which allowed for more flexible and extensive commercial transactions. Credit enabled merchants to purchase goods and services on the promise of future payment, facilitating the growth of trade networks and the development of more complex economic systems. As trade expanded and became more complex, the need for reliable credit information became increasingly important, driving the development of new systems and institutions to manage credit risk.

In the 19th century, merchants and lenders sought ways to evaluate the creditworthiness of potential customers, creating a demand for organized and reliable data to inform their decisions. This need for accurate credit information gave rise to credit bureaus, organizations that would collect, analyze, and distribute financial data to assess individuals' credit risk. The emergence of credit bureaus was a direct response to the growing complexity of commercial transactions and the need for more sophisticated tools to manage credit risk. By providing lenders with reliable credit information, credit bureaus helped to facilitate the expansion of credit markets and the growth of the modern financial system.

The earliest credit bureaus emerged in the mid-1800s in the United States. These organizations primarily operated at a hyper-local level, gathering information from local merchants and public records to create credit reports on individuals. In 1899, the Retail Credit Company (RCC) was founded in Atlanta, Georgia, which would later become Equifax, one of the three major credit bureaus in the United States. RCC initially focused on collecting data related to the insurance industry but soon expanded its scope to include credit information. The early credit bureaus were often small, localized operations that relied on manual data collection and analysis techniques. However, as the demand for credit information grew, these organizations expanded their operations and developed more sophisticated data collection and analysis methods.

Over the years, the credit bureaus began to consolidate and standardize their data collection processes. In 1956, engineer Bill Fair and mathematician Earl Isaac founded Fair, Isaac, and Company, which would later become FICO. They introduced a groundbreaking credit scoring system that used statistical models to predict the likelihood of an individual defaulting on a loan. This approach to credit assessment, which can be considered an early example of data science, enabled the credit bureaus to provide more objective and reliable data to lenders. The development of credit scoring models marked a significant milestone in the evolution of credit bureaus, as it allowed them to provide lenders with a more accurate and consistent measure of credit risk. This, in turn, helped to expand access to credit and support the growth of the modern consumer credit market.

The emergence of computer technology and the internet in the late 20th century significantly revolutionized the operations of credit bureaus, enhancing their data collection and processing capabilities. This transition to digital records and the integration of online data sources allowed for unprecedented access to information, enabling credit bureaus to build more comprehensive and nuanced credit profiles.

Digitization marked a pivotal moment in the expansion of data, leading to an exponential increase in the volume and variety of information available.

While this growth has been instrumental in transforming credit bureaus into vast repositories of financial data, it has also brought critical issues of privacy and inclusivity to the forefront. The ability to amass extensive personal financial data raised significant privacy concerns. It sparked debates over the ethical use of such information, emphasizing the need for robust privacy protections and transparent data handling practices. Concurrently, expanded data collection opened doors for greater inclusivity in credit reporting. By incorporating a broader range of data points, credit bureaus have the potential to provide a more accurate and equitable representation of an individual's creditworthiness, especially for those who have been previously underrepresented or overlooked in traditional credit systems. However, realizing this potential will require credit bureaus to carefully balance the benefits of expanded data collection with the need to protect consumer privacy and ensure fair and unbiased credit assessments. This will likely involve the development of new regulatory frameworks and industry standards to govern the use of personal financial data in credit reporting.

Today, credit bureaus play an essential role in the global financial ecosystem. They use data-driven methodologies to assess credit risk and inform lending decisions. By providing lenders with accurate and timely credit information, credit bureaus help facilitate access to credit for millions of individuals and businesses worldwide. The importance of credit bureaus has only grown in recent years as the global economy has become increasingly interconnected and reliant on credit.

The unique approach of providing a single, easy-to-understand metric—the credit score—instead of raw data or complex datasets can be attributed to the limitations of the technology available during their early years. This approach was a practical solution to data analysis and communication challenges in an era before the widespread adoption of computers and high-speed internet. By distilling complex financial data into a simple, standardized score, credit bureaus were able to provide lenders with a powerful tool for assessing credit risk, even in the absence of advanced data processing technologies.

When credit bureaus first emerged, the internet, advanced computers, databases, big data systems, and cloud computing were not yet in existence. As a result, the bureaus had to find a way to make sense of the financial data they collected and deliver it in a format that was easy for their customers to understand and consume. The credit score was a practical solution to this challenge, enabling the bureaus to deliver actionable insights while overcoming the technological constraints of their time. The development of the credit score was a major innovation that helped revolutionize the credit industry and pave the way for the modern consumer credit market. By providing a simple, standardized measure of credit risk, credit bureaus were able to democratize their data and support the growth of financial institutions.

This focus on delivering a modeled credit score rather than raw data has had several key implications for the functioning of credit bureaus as data companies:

Simplified Decision-Making:

By providing a single metric, credit bureaus made it easier for lenders to assess an applicant's creditworthiness without the need for complex data analysis. This streamlined the credit approval process and helped lenders make more consistent and informed decisions, even with limited technological resources. The simplicity of the credit score also made it easier for consumers to understand their own credit standing and take steps to improve their creditworthiness over time.

Standardization:

The credit score served as a standardized measure of creditworthiness across the industry, allowing lenders to compare applicants on an equal footing despite varying levels of access to technology and data analysis capabilities. This standardization helped to level the playing field for lenders and borrowers alike and supported the growth of a more efficient and equitable credit market.

Accessibility:

The credit score was easily accessible and comprehensible for lenders and consumers during a time when advanced data processing tools were not widely available. This transparency enabled consumers to understand their financial standing better and take steps to improve their creditworthiness, while lenders could quickly assess the risks associated with extending credit.

While the technological landscape has evolved significantly since the early days of credit bureaus, their legacy as data companies that developed a unique solution utilizing the technologies of their time remains relevant. The credit bureaus' hybrid nature as both data companies and score providers highlights the adaptability and ingenuity of data businesses. Their innovative approach to harnessing the power of data transformed the financial industry. It shaped how we interact with credit systems, illustrating the potential of data to create valuable products despite technological constraints. As the data industry continues to evolve and new challenges emerge, the example of the credit bureaus serves as a reminder of the importance of innovation, adaptability, and a focus on delivering value to customers, even in the face of technological limitations. By embracing these principles, data companies can continue to drive progress and shape the future of the industry for years to come.

BLOOMBERG AND THE TERMINAL

Bloomberg L.P., founded in 1981 by Michael Bloomberg and his co-founders Thomas Secunda, Duncan MacMillan, and Charles Zegar, represents an extraordinary story of how a data-driven vision could revolutionize an industry. Their key product, the Bloomberg Terminal, remains indispensable in the financial world, offering unprecedented access to real-time financial data, analytics, and communication tools. The company's success is a testament to the power of data and the transformative impact it can have on an entire industry. Bloomberg's innovative approach to data collection, analysis, and presentation set a new standard for financial information services and inspired countless other data-driven businesses.

Upon leaving his position at Salomon Brothers, Bloomberg was not deterred by the information asymmetry and delayed data that often hampered the financial industry. Instead, he saw an opportunity to fill this information gap. He invested his payout from Salomon Brothers into creating a company that could deliver faster, more accurate financial data to Wall Street. Bloomberg's vision was not just a dream, but a reality rooted in his firsthand experience of the inefficiencies and challenges that financial professionals face in accessing and analyzing critical market data. He recognized that the industry was ripe for disruption and that a data-centric solution could provide a significant competitive advantage to those who embraced it.

In 1982, Bloomberg launched the Market Master terminal, a dedicated computer system that didn't just provide real-time access to market data, financial calculations, and analytics. It revolutionized the way Wall Street operated. This powerful tool allowed traders, brokers, and financial analysts to access and analyze vast amounts of financial data in real-time, dramatically changing the landscape of the financial industry. The Market Master terminal was not just a groundbreaking innovation, but a catalyst for Bloomberg's future success. It demonstrated the immense value of providing financial professionals with instant access to reliable, comprehensive, and actionable data and laid the foundation for developing the iconic Bloomberg Terminal.

However, the real genius behind Bloomberg's success wasn't just creating an innovative platform. Its unique approach to gathering, analyzing, and presenting data set the company apart. Bloomberg understood that the value lay not just in the data itself but in the way it was curated, analyzed, and made accessible to users. Like Playfair, Bloomberg revolutionized how data is visualized and communicated, allowing complex data to be quickly conveyed visually and to people of varying degrees of financial and statistical acumen. Bloomberg's commitment to data visualization and user experience was a critical factor in the widespread adoption of its platform.

At its core, Bloomberg is a quintessential data company. Its primary value proposition was gathering and analyzing publicly available data and consolidating it into a single, easily accessible platform. The company didn't just provide raw data; it offered a comprehensive, data-rich environment that transformed disparate data points into actionable insights. This was the game-changer. By combining various data sources—from real-time market trends and financial data from stock exchanges worldwide to advanced functions for securities valuation, portfolio management, and risk analysis—Bloomberg democratized access to financial data and empowered users to make more informed investment decisions. Bloomberg's ability to integrate and aggregate data from multiple sources was a key differentiator that set it apart. By providing a one-stop shop for financial data and analytics, Bloomberg became an essential tool for investment professionals across the industry.

Bloomberg also extended its data-driven strategy to other business areas, launching Bloomberg News in 1990. By leveraging the company's access to real-time market data, Bloomberg News could provide accurate and timely financial news reports, further enhancing the value of the Bloomberg Terminal. The integration of news and data was a natural extension of Bloomberg's core value proposition, and it helped cement the company's position as a leading provider of financial information.

Bloomberg was able to turn a collection of publicly available information into an indispensable tool for financial professionals by focusing on refining the process of accessing, cleaning, and presenting the data. It became a trusted intermediary, bridging the gap between the raw, often chaotic world of global financial data and the refined, organized, and actionable insights its customers sought. Bloomberg's success highlighted the critical role that data companies can play in the modern economy, inspiring a new generation of data businesses. By demonstrating the value of data curation and analysis, Bloomberg paved the way for the rise of data as a critical asset class and the emergence of data-driven decision-making as a core business tenant.

Despite the evolution of technology and the rise of numerous data companies, Bloomberg's core principle remains relevant today: data is most valuable when it is effectively gathered, analyzed, and presented in a way that users can easily consume and act upon. As we continue to explore the world of data companies, Bloomberg stands as a convincing testament to the power of a data-centric approach. It is an enlightening case study that offers valuable insights into how data can be harnessed to drive innovation, disrupt industries, and create unprecedented value. Bloomberg's success is a reminder that the most successful data companies are those that can effectively bridge the gap between raw data and actionable insights.

Misconceptions: Control vs. Uncertainty

The divergence between data and software companies mirrors a similar divergence in the world of physics. The deterministic nature of classical mechanics runs counter to the inherent uncertainty of quantum mechanics, embodied in Heisenberg's Uncertainty Principle. The two ways of observing the same situation result in entirely different levels of control over the outcome. This analogy serves as a framework for understanding the fundamental differences between data and software companies and the unique challenges and opportunities that each faces in their respective domains.

In the realm of software, predicting outcomes works like classical physics. Once the code is written and the software is deployed, it performs its programmed tasks consistently and predictably, much like a planet faithfully following its orbit. The input, process, and output all fall under the direct control of the software developers and the company. This deterministic operation provides a degree of control different from a data company's operations. Software companies can rely on the stability and reliability of their products as long as the underlying code remains unchanged and the environment in which it operates remains consistent.

On the other hand, data companies operate more similarly to quantum mechanics. Just as Heisenberg's Uncertainty Principle posits that one cannot precisely know both the position and momentum of a particle at the same time, data companies work with a product—data—that they cannot fully predict or control. Data is always a byproduct of something else, be it human behavior, system processes, or natural phenomena. The creation of the data, its evolution over time, and its potential future states remain outside the data company's direct control. This inherent uncertainty presents unique challenges that data companies must navigate, requiring them to adopt a more flexible and adaptive approach to their operations and strategies, constantly monitoring and responding to changes in the data landscape.

Data, in essence, has an intrinsic dynamism that mirrors the unpredictability of reality. This ever-changing nature of data is part of its unique value. It offers a ground-truth reflection of the world's happenings, shifts, and turns, adaptable and ever-responsive to evolving circumstances. Data's ability to capture and reflect the complexities of the real world is what makes it such a powerful tool for insight and decision-making. However, this same dynamism also means that data companies must be prepared to handle the inherent uncertainties and fluctuations that come with working with data.

However, the fluidity that makes data so adaptable and versatile also means its utility and value can fluctuate. Today's invaluable dataset might lose its relevance in the face of unexpected shifts in societal, economic, or industry trends. Data companies must be prepared to pivot and adapt their products and services in response to these changes, constantly seeking new sources of data, and new ways to extract value from existing datasets. This requires a deep understanding of the market and a willingness to embrace uncertainty as a core part of the business model.

For example, before the COVID-19 pandemic, consumer transaction data, much like a well-behaved quantum particle, fell within predictable patterns and was highly correlated with retail company performance. Yet when the pandemic struck, and lockdowns ensued, retail shopping dwindled, and the utility of this data diminished. It was as if the quantum state had collapsed, and the previously reliable data no longer served its purpose. Instead, data on lockdown protocols and local restrictions became the new focus, reflecting the changed reality. This example illustrates the inherent unpredictability of data and the need for data companies to be agile and adaptable in the face of unexpected events.

Data's dual nature—a powerful and versatile pool of insight and its potential for unpredictable changes in utility—presents a unique challenge for data companies. Navigating this inevitable unpredictability is a central aspect of operating in the realm of data, setting it apart from the more deterministic world of software companies.

Unlike software, data does not operate in a vacuum. It is inextricably linked to the complexities and uncertainties of the real world, and data companies must be prepared to navigate this dynamic landscape. This requires a different mindset and approach to product development, business strategy, and risk management, one that embraces uncertainty and adaptability as core principles. By understanding and leveraging the unique properties of data, data companies can unlock new sources of value and drive innovation in ways that software companies simply cannot match.

The Dawn of the Modern Data Company

In the current digital era, both in our personal and professional lives, we find ourselves immersed in a world that thrives on data. The technological advancements of the past few decades have revolutionized how we interact with data, leading to the emergence of a new breed of enterprise: the modern data company. These companies are not just leveraging data as a tool but are built entirely around the collection, analysis, and monetization of data. They represent a fundamental shift in how businesses can operate or create value and are poised to play an increasingly important role in shaping the future of our economy and society.

These entities are built upon transformative elements that have reshaped our world, including sweeping digitization, the advent of the internet, the rise of cloud computing, and the evolution of big data technology. Each of these elements has contributed to the creation of a new data ecosystem, one that is characterized by unprecedented scale, complexity, and dynamism.

The far-reaching digitization of our lives—from banking transactions and emails to shopping habits and smartphone usage—has led to an extraordinary volume of data. This sea of information, once inaccessible or non-existent, now forms the bedrock of countless data-driven solutions, insights, and innovations. This data is the raw material that modern data companies use to create value.

Simultaneously, the internet has not only accelerated the digitization process but also connected the world in unprecedented ways. This global network has made data readily accessible and shareable, breaking down geographical and temporal barriers and enabling the instantaneous transmission and receipt of information.

Likewise, cloud computing has fundamentally changed the way data is stored and processed. It has shifted the paradigm from localized servers to distributed, scalable systems that can handle massive volumes of data in real-time. This shift has significantly reduced the cost and complexity of data storage and processing, making it feasible for even small startups to leverage big data.

The evolution of big data technology has revolutionized how we analyze and derive insights from data. Tools and techniques like machine learning, AI, and advanced analytics can now process and interpret complex and voluminous datasets, providing valuable insights that drive decision-making and strategy. These technologies have opened up new possibilities for data companies to create value from data and develop new products and services previously unimaginable.

The confluence of these factors has not only given rise to a wealth of new opportunities for data startups that have yet to be imagined but has also transformed existing enterprises. It has allowed us to reimagine the boundaries of what is possible with data, catalyzing a new era of data-driven innovation. The modern data company is at the forefront of this transformation and is well-positioned to lead the way in creating new value from data. As data becomes an increasingly critical asset for businesses and society as a whole, the role of the modern data company will only continue to grow in importance.

THE THREE KEY ELEMENTS OF MODERN DATA COMPANIES

Modern data companies are distinguished by three elements that serve as the cornerstone of their operations and strategy. These keys are foundational to the operational framework, competitive strategy, and success of today's data-driven enterprises. Together, they form the nodes of The Virtuous Cycle of data economies: more data leads to better products, which attract more users, who in turn generate more data. At a more granular level, which we'll explore below, this means that if companies can collect data at scale, they can monetize it in increasingly innovative ways. In turn, data companies will get more customers who will generate more data, contributing to the company's competitive edge in the industry.

The path to establishing a data company is marked by considerable cost and effort, with the pivotal challenge being the accumulation of a critical mass of data. Once this threshold is reached, the firm is poised to deliver valuable insights and services. This milestone also triggers a decrease in the marginal cost of additional data acquisition, leading to substantial economies of scale. Dominant data companies can leverage this dynamic to provide superior services at competitive prices, reinforcing their market dominance. As a data company grows and acquires more data, it becomes increasingly difficult for competitors to catch up, creating a powerful competitive moat. The Three Key Elements of a Modern Data Company are as follows:

Data collection at scale:

The digitization of virtually all aspects of our daily lives has unlocked data collection at scale. From online banking transactions and eCommerce shopping to social media interactions, satellite imagery, and smartphone usage, today's data companies can amass data on an unprecedented scale and rate. The ability to collect data at scale is a critical success factor for modern data companies, as it provides the raw material needed to generate valuable insights and drive innovation.

Explicit Data Monetization Strategy:

An explicit data monetization strategy is a focused approach where monetizing data is prioritized as a primary objective within an organization's operations. This approach positions data monetization not as a secondary or incidental outcome but as a central strategic goal. Despite its inherent value, raw data is akin to an uncut diamond—it needs the right processes and context to unlock its true worth. Modern data companies are masters of transforming these raw data assets into actionable insights, personalized experiences, and innovative products and services, extracting value and monetizing their vast data repositories.

Winner-take-all market dynamics:

The company that can collect the most data and extract the most value from it often dominates, leaving little room for competitors. This winner-take-all dynamic is a key feature of many modern data markets, and it creates a powerful incentive for data companies to invest heavily upfront in data collection and analysis. In many cases, the first company to achieve critical mass in a particular data market can quickly establish a dominant position, making it difficult for competitors to gain a foothold.

In the following sections, we will explore each of these key elements, from their practical implications to their impact on a data company's trajectory. Whether you are an aspiring entrepreneur planning to launch a data startup or an established business leader aiming to leverage data within your current operations, understanding these elements will provide valuable insights into the mechanics and strategies of modern data companies.

DATA COLLECTION AT SCALE: FUEL FOR MODERN DATA COMPANIES

In the arena of modern data companies, scale plays a critical role. Every online purchase, digital interaction, social media engagement, or smartphone notification contributes to a rapidly expanding reservoir of data. This could be user-generated content, behavioral data, transactional data, or machine-generated data—all fueling the data companies' engines. And by scale, we mean that this data is not just accumulated, it's compounded. It's not thrown away; it's recycled and reused indefinitely. Consider how Ancestry.com built an empire on old bureaucratic documents like ship manifests and government-building visitor logs, showcasing the transformative power of scale in data collection.

The size of data collection in the context of a modern data company is not merely a matter of accumulating vast numbers but also about the depth of data. Depth refers to the level of detail or granularity the data provides about user behaviors, preferences, and trends. Data companies today can capture this granular detail at an unprecedented scale. This isn't just about collecting different data types but amassing a particular kind of data, be it transaction records, customer profiles, or user-generated content, on a massive scale. The distinguishing factor of modern data companies is their capacity to collect detailed information in a high-volume, high-velocity data environment, enabling them to build a rich, nuanced, and comprehensive understanding of their target domains.

This level of detail is a formidable tool for understanding and predicting user behavior, tailoring products and services, and driving business decisions. It is the scale that provides the 'ground truth.' Unlike survey or polling companies that infer insights from a subset of the population, data companies can access the reality of the situation due to the sheer volume of data they collect. This critical mass of data not only provides reliable, fact-based insights but also instills confidence in the decision-making process, as these insights can be actioned directly without the need for extrapolation or assumption.

In the next section, we will consider how these companies leverage this rich data source and transform it into valuable products and services through explicit data monetization strategies. For now, it is essential to recognize the sheer scale of data collection today—a key factor that powers the operations of modern data companies, propelling them towards success. The ability to collect and analyze data at scale is not just a technical capability but a fundamental shift in the way businesses operate and compete. As data becomes an increasingly critical asset for companies across all industries, those that can effectively leverage the power of data at scale will be well-positioned to thrive.

EXPLICIT DATA MONETIZATION STRATEGIES: THE MODERN DATA COMPANY'S SUPERCHARGER

In the past, data was a means to an end, typically employed to deliver a specific use case or an end-to-end solution. Data was seen as a tool to enable a particular function or to solve a specific problem rather than as a valuable asset in its own right. This narrow view of data's potential limited the ways in which it could be monetized and the value that could be extracted from it.

Data companies such as credit bureaus served as gatekeepers of specific, highly curated data sets that they would monetize by selling comprehensive solutions based on this data—for instance, a credit score that encapsulated an individual's credit risk. In these cases, the product was the score itself, an endpoint derived from the data rather than access to the underlying data.

The landscape has dramatically shifted in the era of modern data companies. Today, data itself is often the primary product. Rather than focusing on delivering a single, comprehensive solution, modern data companies provide access to vast and continually updated data sets that end users can navigate and manipulate themselves. These companies recognize that the value of data lies not just in its immediate application but in its potential for a myriad of uses to which they might not be privy. This shift in mindset has opened up new opportunities for data monetization and enabled data companies to create value in ways previously unimaginable.

An explicit data monetization strategy in a modern data company centers around selling data access. This access could be direct, through selling raw, unprocessed data, or indirect, through API access or through a platform that allows users to analyze and manipulate the data to their needs. The value proposition lies in the data's breadth, depth, and freshness and the insights that can be extracted from it. By providing access to their data assets, modern data companies enable their customers to derive value in ways that are tailored to their specific needs and use cases.

This shift from selling solutions to selling data access has led to democratizing data usage. Instead of being confined to a single purpose, data can now be used, reused, and repurposed in countless ways by the end users, sparking innovation and driving value across a spectrum of industries and applications. The democratization of data has also led to the emergence of new business models and revenue streams for data companies. By providing access to their data assets, these companies can tap into a much larger market and create value for a wider range of customers and industries.

WINNER-TAKE-ALL MARKET DYNAMICS: THE FASTEST ENGINE WINS

Data companies operate in an environment where the value of their products increases with their volume and variety. The more data a data company has, the more comprehensive and valuable the insights it offers can be. This creates a powerful network effect: as a company acquires more data, its services become more valuable to users, which in turn attracts more users, which then generates even more data. A good example is business prospect software, such as Zoom Info and Apollo Sales, which boast prominently about how many business contacts are in their database on their websites. This self-reinforcing cycle creates a strong incentive for data companies to prioritize data acquisition and to invest heavily in building and maintaining their data assets.

This dominance is not guaranteed or static. It is contingent upon continuous data acquisition. If an early leader becomes complacent and slows the pace of data collection, it risks losing its competitive edge. New market entrants, eager to challenge the status quo, can seize this opportunity to accumulate data rapidly and pose a serious threat to the incumbent. This dynamic creates constant pressure for data companies to innovate and evolve as they seek to stay ahead of the competition and maintain their market position. It also means that the most successful data companies are often those that are able to sustain a high rate of data acquisition over time, even as they grow and mature.

The 'winner-take-all' market dynamic, while potent, is not without its perils. It can potentially stifle competition as emerging players strive to establish a foothold in markets already dominated by data giants. Above all, users demand stability and continuity in their data flows, insisting on unwavering assurances that their data access will remain uninterrupted and dependable. This dynamic is also a paradox. It fuels innovation and efficiency, yet it also poses the risk of creating monopolies and stifling market diversity. Modern data companies, therefore, confront the intricate challenge of navigating this delicate dynamic.

In Review:

- **Exploration of Data Company Evolution:** We traced the journey of data companies from ancient civilizations to the modern era, highlighting how technological advancements revolutionized data collection and analysis.

- **Definition of Modern Data Companies:** We described modern data companies as entities that utilize data as their primary asset, offering advanced analytics, unique data sets, and AI-driven decision-making tools.

- **Focus on Ethics in Data Management:** We emphasized the importance of ethical considerations in data use, including privacy, security, and fairness in data handling.

- **Technological Milestones in Data Evolution:** We outlined key technological developments like microchips, computers, and the internet that have transformed how data is created, stored, processed, and analyzed.

- **Strategic Role of Data Companies:** We discussed the transition of data companies from basic analytics providers to strategic business partners, leveraging big data, AI, and machine learning.

- **Historical Overview of Data:** We provided an overview of the history of data, from early civilizations to the present, highlighting how data management has mirrored societal and technological progress.

- **Data Collection Methods in Ancient Civilizations:** We explored data collection methods in ancient societies like Babylon, the Incas, the Egyptians, and the Romans, demonstrating how data influenced societal prosperity and stability.

- **Insights on Data Analysis in the Industrial Revolution:** We highlighted the contributions of early statisticians during the Industrial Revolution to modern data analysis and visualization techniques.

CHAPTER 2
FROM RAW MATERIAL
TO REFINED PRODUCT

FROM RAW MATERIAL TO REFINED PRODUCT

It's time to focus on data companies' critical yet complex responsibility: 'productizing' the data for commercial use. This process, called data productization, is a significant cornerstone in a data company's foundation. It involves the transformation of raw, unstructured, and often overwhelming volumes of data into consumable, valuable insights. Data productization is not a one-time event but an ongoing process that requires continuous refinement and adaptation to meet the evolving needs of customers, the market, and the data itself. It is a critical function distinguishing successful data companies from those struggling to create value from their data assets.

Unlike a software product, where value is directly tied to features and functions, the value in a data product springs from its potential to answer questions, solve problems, and yield insights that empower decision-making. This potential is only unleashed when the data is manipulated, structured, and presented in a way that is readily accessible and usable to customers. It is not about the quality of the data, per se, but the insights it can reveal.

4 Vital Tasks for Data Productization

In this chapter, we will examine the journey from data collection to delivery to better understand the process of data productization. We will probe strategic considerations, potential hurdles, and the tactics data companies can employ to successfully turn raw data into a commercial product—and a successful company. Through a series of four vital tasks, we will provide a comprehensive framework for data productization that can be adapted to suit the unique needs and goals of your data company. Whether you are just starting out or looking to optimize your existing data products, these tasks will provide valuable insights and practical guidance to help you succeed.

VITAL TASK 1: HARNESSING THE 'JOBS TO BE DONE' FRAMEWORK:

We will apply Clayton Christensen's renowned business model to the world of data products, helping you identify the needs your data product should fulfill to meet the customer's needs. By understanding the specific 'jobs' your customers are trying to accomplish, you can design data products that are tailored to their unique requirements and deliver real value.

VITAL TASK 2: ENHANCE THE DATA TO EXPAND MARKETS:

We will examine ways to augment your data with feature enhancements, dimensions, measures, Named Entity Recognition (NER), and more. We will also explore how data enhancements can create valuable links between different data sets, multiplying the potential use cases. Expanding the scope and depth of your data can open up new markets and create new growth opportunities.

VITAL TASK 3: PACKAGE THE DATA:

We will discuss how to package your data optimally to cater to different clients, industries, verticals, and markets. This includes considerations such as data format, delivery methods, and pricing models. By tailoring your data products to your target customers' specific needs and preferences, you can increase adoption and maximize the value of your data assets.

VITAL TASK 4: VALIDATE THE DATA:

Finally, we will guide you through the process of verifying the representativeness and accuracy of your data and determining its fidelity to ground truth. This is a critical step in ensuring the reliability and credibility of your data products, and it requires rigorous testing and validation processes. By investing in data validation, you can build trust with your customers and establish your data products as the gold standard in your industry.

By the end of this chapter, you'll have a holistic understanding of data productization and be able to use these insights and strategies to navigate the rewarding expedition from raw data to revenue. With this knowledge in hand, you'll be well-equipped to create data products that deliver real value to your customers and drive the growth and success of your data company. Remember, data productization is an ongoing process that requires continuous refinement and adaptation, so be prepared to iterate and evolve as you learn and grow.

Vital Task 1: Harnessing the 'Jobs to be Done' Framework

In the realm of product development, few concepts have been as influential as the 'Jobs to be Done' framework. Originated by innovation expert Tony Ulwick, this customer-centric model was later popularized by renowned Harvard Business School professor Clayton Christensen.

The 'Jobs to be Done' framework maintains that customers hire products or services to perform specific jobs or tasks. For example, a customer doesn't buy a drill for the sake of owning a drill but because they need to create a hole. Therefore, the job to be done is to make a hole, not buy a drill. This framework results in a paradigm shift from product features to customer needs. It encourages product developers to understand the why behind a purchase, fostering a deeper understanding of what customers genuinely need and value.

HOW IS THE 'JOBS TO BE DONE' FRAMEWORK RELEVANT TO DATA PRODUCTIZATION?

For data companies, the jobs customers need to accomplish usually revolve around decision-making. Customers rely on data products to gain insights, answer questions, predict outcomes, or discern trends. They hire the data to inform and enhance their decisions across a myriad of fields like marketing, finance, operations, and more.

The 'Jobs to be Done' framework proves highly beneficial for data product development as it urges data companies to think beyond the mere attributes of their data. Rather than focusing on the data itself (like transaction data or social media data), the 'Jobs to be Done' approach inspires data companies to consider what the data can accomplish for the customer.

For instance, a marketing team might hire social media data not out of interest in the data per se, but to understand consumer sentiments about their brand. In this scenario, the 'Job to be Done' is not supplying social media data but revealing consumer sentiments.

This shift in perspective significantly influences how a data company collects, processes, packages, and presents its data. It guides the data enhancement process, indicating which features, measures, or tools will make the data more adept at accomplishing its job. It can also inform marketing, sales, and service strategies, ensuring that all aspects of the data company align with a customer's needs.

CASE STUDY: APPLYING THE 'JOBS TO BE DONE' FRAMEWORK TO A CONSUMER TRANSACTION DATA COMPANY – FOCUSING ON RETAIL

This case study takes you behind the scenes of a real-life consumer transaction data company that was wrestling with the challenge of productizing data. We've added a pinch of dramatization to enliven the narrative a bit. Guided by the 'Jobs to be Done' framework, we explore the labyrinth of consumer behavior, unearthing hidden insights and reshaping raw data into valuable products.

Consider Facteus, the company Jonathan co-founded and where Lorn led product and corporate strategy. Facteus specializes in collecting and curating consumer transaction and spending data. Despite its data's richness, Facteus struggled to fully connect with its retail customers and the greater retail industry. To address this, they applied the 'Jobs to be Done' framework to better understand their customers' needs and enhance their products accordingly.

Despite the powerful nature of Facteus' offering, it struggled to convert retail prospects into paying customers. In fact, those who did not buy struggled to articulate exactly why or what might make the data more useful for them. While essential, the raw data and sales process did not illuminate these prospective customers' deeper needs and pain points. This realization sparked a revelation for the Facteus team.

Rather than only offering access to raw transaction data, the company needed to think more deeply about the 'jobs' their data was being hired to do. The data had to be more than simply accurate and comprehensive—it needed to be relevant, insightful, and actionable. It needed to help retailers answer their most pressing questions, solve their most challenging problems, and seize their most promising opportunities. This realization was a game-changer for Facteus, and the 'Jobs to be Done' framework provided the blueprint for this new approach to product development.

To address this change in perspective, the Facteus team first turned to their existing retail customers. Through a series of in-depth interviews, they sought to uncover the jobs these businesses were hiring the data to perform. As the team sifted through the responses, they began to see a pattern. Retailers were keenly interested in the tectonic shifts in consumer behavior, namely the pendulum swing between in-person and online shopping and the rising influence of delivery platforms in this digital revolution.

While this insight was helpful, the Facteus team also recognized that their existing customer base might not encompass the broader retail landscape they hoped to appeal to. To capture a wider perspective and to reinforce their confidence in their findings, the team leveraged industry-leading expert networks, collecting insights that painted a more comprehensive picture of the retail industry's needs. The findings reiterated their initial discoveries, validating the need for a more granular understanding of the changing consumer spending habits and the burgeoning role of delivery platforms (e.g. Uber Eats, Shipt, etc).

While the wider net only resulted in further validation in this instance, taking the time to confirm data findings through an overarching industry perspective is an essential step in the process. It might not always be the case that your existing customers have the same concerns as the broader potential customer base.

The first job Facteus identified was understanding the shift between online and in-person shopping. In response, Facteus developed a new dimension to their data that clearly delineated whether a transaction was made online or in person. This allowed retailers to analyze consumer behavior and spending patterns within these two distinct channels, giving them the insights needed to adjust their strategies accordingly.

Next came the task of discerning the impact of delivery platforms on consumer spending. Retailers were keen to comprehend how services like Instacart, UberEats, Grubhub, Postmates, and Shipt were reshaping consumer purchasing behavior. In response to this need, Facteus made sure to include these delivery platforms in their existing Named Entity Recognition (NER) process, thus identifying transactions associated with these services. This enriched dimension of data offered their retail customers a valuable lens through which they could better understand the role of these burgeoning delivery platforms in the ever-changing retail landscape.

Embracing the 'Jobs to be Done' framework enabled Facteus to transform their product to better resonate with their customers' needs. They evolved beyond merely distributing raw transaction data to communicating actionable insights specifically tailored for the retail industry. The value of their product was no longer confined to its inherent attributes. Now, it was shaped by the jobs it could fulfill for its clients.

This customer-centric paradigm shift not only improved their existing product but also expanded their market reach within the retail industry. By adding these features, they could address a broader array of use cases and solve more of the pressing questions being asked in the retail market. This led to not only increased customer satisfaction but also an uptick in sales and market share.

Misconceptions: Product Development – Architects & Builders vs. Miners & Refiners

In a software company, product development is typically a structured and linear process. The development team sets out to build a product with a well-defined set of features, capabilities, and interfaces. The product roadmap is often established early on, outlining the key milestones, feature additions, and enhancements the team plans to deliver over time.

Alternatively, data companies do not construct their offerings out of the blue but collect, curate, and provide access to their product: data. If software development works like construction—building a product from the ground up—then data companies are more like miners working with raw materials and procuring, refining, enhancing, and coming up with new uses as the market demands.

This enhancement process is a critical part of product development in a data company. It does not change the underlying data but amplifies its value by enabling it to answer more complex questions and serve a broader range of use cases. For instance, a company might enhance the granularity of geo-tagging for each transaction in a consumer spending data set.

This enhanced data can then interact or overlay with other data sets, such as weather data, allowing for more comprehensive analyses. It opens new possibilities, like correlating precipitation levels with reduced sales but an increase in drive-thrus for coffee. Such enhancements are so transformative that they can create new markets and opportunities for the data.

The data company does not build the data product in the same way a software company builds its software. Instead, it reveals and enriches the data product by extracting, cleaning, integrating, enhancing, and structuring the data in ways that make its inherent value accessible and usable. It is less about creation and control and more about exploration, discovery, enhancement, and presentation.

THREE OTHER JOBS FOR DATA

While the Facteus case study provides a glimpse into the
application of the Jobs to be Done framework, the potential
jobs for data differ across industries, organizations, and
use cases. To further inspire you, let's explore some less
conventional ways data can be hired to do a 'job':

Understanding Trends:

Picture a grocery chain looking to optimize its inventory.
They might hire data not just from their own sales systems
but also from broader sources such as health and wellness
trends, regional dietary habits, and even agricultural reports.
With this data, they can predict emerging food trends, adapt
their inventory accordingly, and cater to evolving consumer
tastes and preferences.

Forecasting Events:

Picture a ride-sharing company that wants to hire weather
data to forecast demand surges. By combining historical ride
data with weather patterns, they can predict when inclement
weather might lead to a spike in ride requests. This helps
them manage supply-demand dynamics more effectively,
ensuring customer satisfaction while optimizing driver
availability.

Deep Dives:

Envision a real estate developer contemplating the location of a new residential complex. They could hire data on urban green spaces, local school ratings, crime statistics, and even coffee shop densities. This less-obvious data can offer a comprehensive understanding of the attractiveness of different neighborhoods, thereby influencing their decision on where to build and demonstrating the practicality of unconventional data use.

Vital Task 2: Enhance the Data to Expand Markets

We compared the process of data product development in data companies to mining for precious metals or gems. The raw data plays the role of a rugged mountain full of unrefined minerals, and the data company's job is to excavate, refine, and fashion these raw materials into something of value—a polished gem ready for market. This section will take us deeper into the mine to understand the mechanisms, tools, and skill sets needed to refine and process these elements.

Data enhancement is a transformative process product development pipeline that can revolutionize the way a data company operates. Adding just one dimension or feature to a dataset can turn a good product into a great one. Here, we will carefully consider the specifics of data enhancement, including feature enhancements, measures, and a powerful tool called Named Entity Recognition (NER). We'll explore how these techniques can augment and enrich your data, transforming it from a raw input into a high-value output. We will continue using Facteus to illustrate the power of data enhancement in the productization journey.

GEOLOCATION DATA ENHANCEMENT

While rich in information, Facteus' consumer cardholder transaction data comes in an unstructured format and often lacks clear geographical context. A sample data record might look like this:

Transaction ID: 123456789
Transaction Date: 2023-05-01
Transaction Time: 09:30 AM
Retailer: COFFEE SHOP 1
Transaction Details: STARPEET COFFEE SHOP 1 5TH AVE NY

Total Expenditure: $5.50

While seemingly just a string of text, the "Transaction Details" field holds valuable geo-information that can be mined for data enhancement. Recognizing this potential, Facteus developed a process to extract the location details embedded within the text string of "Transaction Details." This raw, unstructured information was transformed into a structured geolocation data point. For instance, the text string 'COFFEE SHOP 1 5TH AVE NY' could be enhanced to add structured geolocation data:

Geolocation: {
   "Store Name": "STARPEET COFFEE SHOP 1",
   "Street": "5TH AVE",
   "City": "NY",
}

This enhancement completely changed the game. The newly created geolocation data served as a 'join key.' A join key is a concept popularized by data industry thought leader and entrepreneur Auren Hoffman, defined as data fields that connect existing datasets and provide new contexts to existing data. They allow transaction data to link with other datasets and concepts.

Facteus' geolocation information now correlates the transaction data with weather data or events data.

Questions like, "Was there a recent spike in coffee shop sales due to a heat wave?" or "Did a local event like a TED Talk influence spending patterns at nearby stores?" could now be answered.

This process of enhancing raw data with geolocation information transformed Facteus' dataset from an unstructured collection of transaction details into a multi-dimensional resource. It revealed patterns and insights that were previously hidden, paving the way for many data jobs and providing more profound insights into consumer behavior and the environmental factors influencing spending.

TEMPORAL DATA ENHANCEMENT

Facteus introduced a temporal (time-based) dimension to further enhance its transaction data. The company structured the raw date and time information into more detailed components: year, month, day of the week, time of the day, and season.

This temporal data served as another join key, connecting the transaction data to other time-related datasets or concepts. For instance, by linking the transaction data with holiday data, Facteus could explore questions such as, "Do customers spend more on certain items during the holiday season?" or "Is there a spike in transactions at toy stores on Saturdays?"

Additionally, by correlating the transaction data with economic indicators, Facteus could explicate how macroeconomic factors influence spending patterns. Temporal data transformed the transaction data into a dynamic resource. It revealed patterns and insights that were previously hidden, fulfilled a variety of jobs, and provided a deeper understanding of how consumer behavior changes over time.

UNLEASHING POTENTIAL: BROADENING HORIZONS WITH DATA ENHANCEMENTS

It's worth taking a moment to consider other potential data enhancements across different types of data. The process we've seen in the Facteus case study—of extracting and structuring valuable information from raw data to create additional dimensions—is not confined to transaction data. Let's briefly explore a few more examples to spark your creativity and inspire new possibilities.

Fitness App Data:

Imagine a company that collects fitness app data, tracking metrics like daily steps, heart rate, sleep patterns, and food intake. This rich, though raw, dataset could be enhanced by adding a patient's medical history or genetic data. For instance, by integrating genetic data—information about predispositions to specific health conditions—into the fitness app's dataset, we've created a powerful join key.

This enhancement introduces a whole new realm of personalized healthcare possibilities by connecting fitness data to healthcare providers or health-focused AI algorithms. By combining these data sets, healthcare professionals or algorithms can offer more personalized advice or interventions based on an individual's lifestyle and genetic predispositions.

Consider a scenario where the data indicates a genetic predisposition to heart disease and a consistent pattern of saturated fat intake. In this case, a personalized intervention could be designed to assist the user in reducing their consumption and managing their potential heart disease risk.

However, the benefits of this data enhancement don't stop there. If the fitness app data shows a sedentary lifestyle or lack of sufficient physical activity, personalized fitness programs could also be suggested to the user to improve their physical activity levels, thus helping to regulate blood pressure and lower their chance of heart disease.

Integrating fitness app data with other health data creates a more proactive, tailored, and comprehensive approach to healthcare. It allows healthcare providers and individuals alike to be ahead of the curve, taking informed steps toward disease prevention and health improvement.

Social Media Data:

A company that specializes in social media data has a goldmine of information at its disposal. The raw data contains information about the user, the content of posts, timestamps, likes, shares, and more. However, there is an even deeper layer of information that can be extracted from the text itself: sentiment.

Using natural language processing techniques, the company could analyze the text of each post to assign a sentiment score, categorizing each post as positive, negative, or neutral. This sentiment score serves as a powerful join key, providing the potential to correlate social media trends with other datasets.

For example, linking sentiment scores with stock market data could illuminate the impact of public sentiment on market trends. Similarly, correlating sentiment scores with event data could provide insights into public reactions to major events.

Taking this a step further, we could incorporate timestamps into our sentiment analysis. This would allow us to gauge public sentiment in response to specific periods or events.

A powerful example of this would be analyzing the sentiment of tweets or messages during the COVID-19 lockdown periods. Substantial evidence showed that mental health deteriorated for many during lockdown. By correlating this timeframe with a potential influx of negative sentiment on social media, the data can support this hypothesis and offer another data point for understanding public mental health trends during the pandemic.

By adding sentiment scoring to enhance raw social media data, the potential applications become considerably more varied and valuable, from monitoring public mental health trends to predicting market movements.

Transportation Data:

Imagine a company that specializes in the collection and analysis of transportation data. Its raw data includes specific ride details such as GPS coordinates, start and end times, passenger count, and fare, among others. While the data in its raw form is already insightful, the company could use specific longitude and latitude coordinates as a 'join key' to enhance its value further.

These coordinates could be used to link their ride data to Point-of-Interest (POI) data sets. This would allow the company to understand where most traffic or rides occur. Are certain restaurants or entertainment venues causing high traffic during specific times? Such data could be valuable to city planners or even the venues themselves.

Additionally, the company could use these specific geographic coordinates to connect with an Events database. This would enable the company to analyze the impact of various city events on the transportation system. Do concerts lead to a spike in rides in certain areas? Does a sports event cause increased traffic congestion? Such insights could help event organizers and city transportation departments plan more effectively.

By using geographic coordinates as a join key, the company can enrich its transportation data, linking it with POI or Events data to provide deeper insights into the dynamics of city transportation. This illustrates how enhancing data can broaden its applicability and potential for analysis, opening opportunities for more sophisticated and meaningful queries.

DATA ENHANCEMENTS AS PATHWAYS TO MARKET EXPANSION

When we enhance data, we are not only improving its quality and utility but also creating new opportunities, markets, and avenues for growth. By strategically enhancing data, companies can broaden their target audience, enter new industries, and forge powerful partnerships.

Facteus transformed transaction data, initially valuable primarily to asset managers, into a strategic tool for retail site selection by enhancing it with geolocation and temporal attributes. This tangible example demonstrates how data enhancements can create new opportunities and markets for a data company.

The second enhancement Facteus introduced was the Retailer Category. By classifying each transaction into specific product categories, such as electronics, groceries, or fashion, based on the retailer's primary business, the transaction data was also transformed into a powerful tool for market research firms.

Market researchers found immense value in this new dimension. They could now track spending trends in specific categories, gauge the popularity of various product types, and assess the performance of different retailers within each category. This data not only informed marketing strategies and guided product development but also influenced pricing decisions. For instance, if the data showed a surge in spending on organic groceries, a grocery chain could react by expanding its organic product line to capitalize on this trend. In both examples, Facteus unlocked new markets by adding strategic enhancements to its data.

Misconceptions: Tools vs. Clay

Software companies are akin to hand tools. They are built to address very specific problems or complete specialized tasks. The value proposition is often deterministic, meaning that each customer uses the software to address the same or similar use cases. For instance, customer relationship management (CRM) software is used by various companies to manage and analyze customer interactions and data to improve business relationships, customer retention, and drive sales growth. Regardless of the industry or size of the company, CRM software serves the same fundamental purpose.

In contrast, data companies are more akin to unshaped clay—moldable and adaptable to a wide array of use cases. They provide base material (data) that can be shaped, analyzed, and interpreted in countless ways to serve diverse needs. The same data set can be used to address many different problems, depending on the user's perspective, industry, and specific requirements.

Take, for instance, a data company providing consumer transaction data. This data set can be used by a retailer for site selection, determining where to open or close stores based on consumer spending habits in different areas. Meanwhile, another retailer might use the same data set to analyze competition, studying spending patterns to understand the strengths and weaknesses of their competitors in different regions. On the other hand, a hedge fund might use the very same transaction data to inform its investment strategy, utilizing the information to predict market trends and make investment decisions.

The malleable nature of data sits at the core of data companies. Not unlike clay being crafted into various forms by a skilled artisan, this raw material can be transformed, refashioned, and repurposed to suit an array of distinct applications. This inherent flexibility is a key differentiator between data companies and software companies.

The unique value propositions, operational strategies, and potential of data companies stem from the inherent adaptability of data. Like an artist recognizing the myriad possibilities within a block of clay, a data company sees an opportunity within a dataset. This subtle yet profound understanding forms a significant divergence from the deterministic applications typical of software companies.

Acknowledging this difference is essential to fully appreciate the expansive scope and transformative power of data companies.

Vital Task 3: Package the Data

While the terms 'data enhancement' and 'data packaging' might seem similar, they serve very different functions. Data enhancement is about enriching the data and adding layers of information to make it more valuable and insightful. In contrast, data packaging focuses on presenting this enhanced data in a manner that is most beneficial and convenient to the user.

Like any product on the market, packaging can significantly impact its appeal and utility. A beautifully wrapped gift creates anticipation and delight even before it's opened; the same principle applies to data. If your data is well-packaged, it becomes easier for your clients to consume, understand, and extract insights.

Packaging data involves considering how the data will be used and who will be using it. It's about formatting, structuring, and presenting your data to meet the specific needs of different clients, industries, verticals, and markets. It's also about making your data accessible and user-friendly, ensuring that clients can easily interact with and extract value from your data product.

TAILORING DATA PACKAGES FOR DIFFERENT CLIENT NEEDS

Consider the case of a systematic quantitative hedge fund. In this high-stakes, fast-paced environment, the fund requires the most detailed raw data possible. The data's job is to feed sophisticated algorithms that are designed to predict and capitalize on tiny market shifts. Given this, the hedge fund doesn't need prepackaged summaries or reports. They require the raw data in its most granular form for their custom analysis. These clients need high-frequency data feeds on a daily basis. They already have the necessary infrastructure and expertise to handle and process this raw, high-volume data.

On the other hand, there's the traditional brick-and-mortar retailer. Their goal is to understand how the emergence of online delivery apps has influenced their business. Unlike the hedge fund, they aren't equipped to process and analyze vast amounts of raw data. They need the data packaged into digestible, understandable formats—bite-sized summaries, graphical reports, and interactive dashboards.

This retailer isn't looking for a daily feed of raw data. Instead, they want a comprehensive monthly or quarterly report that breaks down the trends and provides clear, actionable insights. They may not have a team of data scientists at their disposal, but they do have keen business acumen and an understanding of their market. The data product they need is one that aligns with their business operations, helping them make strategic decisions about store operations, marketing, and product offerings.

While the underlying data for these two client types may be the same, their packaging needs are starkly different. This is where the art of data packaging shines. It's about delivering the data in the form that's most advantageous, accessible, and useful for the client, thereby optimizing its value and impact. The significance of tailoring data packages to suit client needs cannot be overstated. It is the key to maximizing the data's usefulness and ensuring client satisfaction.

IMPACT OF PACKAGING ON PRODUCT DEVELOPMENT AND TEAM COMPOSITION

Different packaging strategies not only shape the final product but also dictate the approach to product development and the skills required to execute it effectively.

When catering to a client like a systematic quantitative hedge fund, the product development focus lies primarily on data extraction, processing, and delivery. Building a reliable and secure infrastructure to handle large amounts of raw data efficiently is paramount. It's a highly technical discipline requiring strong engineering foundations: data accuracy, integrity, delivery speed, and system reliability.

The core team would typically comprise data engineers, cloud engineers, and database administrators. They would ensure that the high-frequency data feeds are generated and transmitted without fail. While the user interface may be a minor concern for such clients, the complexity of raw data necessitates technically proficient customer support, which can assist clients with integration and troubleshooting issues.

Conversely, product development shifts its focus if the client is a traditional retailer looking for ready-made insights. Here, the emphasis shifts towards data analysis, insight generation, and user interface design. Data must be transformed into meaningful metrics, visualized effectively, and delivered in an intuitive, easy-to-navigate format. Product features could include dashboards, trend analyses, and alert systems to highlight significant changes in data.

This demands a different team structure. While technical roles remain essential, the team would also need data analysts or scientists to extract insights and UX/UI designers to create an accessible interface. Customer support in this context would need to understand the business implications of the data and guide clients in applying these insights to their decision-making process.

In both scenarios, the product management role evolves to meet the packaging requirements. For raw data products, the product manager would likely need a strong technical background to navigate data accuracy and system reliability. For packaged insights, the product manager would need to blend business acumen with user empathy, focusing on delivering clear, actionable insights in a user-friendly package.

The packaging strategy not only influences the end product but also dictates the direction of product development and the composition of the team executing it. Recognizing and addressing these differences can help data companies tailor their approach to meet diverse client needs, ensuring a product that is not just technically sound but also performs the specific job that the data is hired to do.

PACKAGING DATA STRATEGICALLY

How data is packaged is a strategic decision that impacts product development, resource allocation, team composition, and, ultimately, a data company's overall trajectory.

Developing a variety of data packages is an appealing proposition on the surface. It caters to a broad range of clients, each with unique needs and preferences. However, beneath this enticing prospect lies a complex and resource-intensive process. Building out multiple data packaging products requires considerable investment in terms of technology, talent, and time.

Embarking on such a course doesn't come with a guarantee of widespread adoption. A data package that works excellently for one client may be unsuitable for another. Misaligned or poorly executed data products could lead to client dissatisfaction and potential churn, ultimately failing to generate the intended return on investment.

Therefore, the early decisions about which data packages to build and which to pass over are critical for a data startup. Such decisions should not be based on hypothetical scenarios or speculative demand. Instead, they need to be grounded in a deep understanding of the target customers, their 'Jobs to be Done,' and the practical limitations of the startup's resources.

The chosen packaging strategy will set the course for the entire company, shaping the development of its product offerings, the hiring strategy, and even corporate culture. It will determine whether the company takes a more technically focused path by catering to clients who crave raw, granular data or adopts a business-focused approach by developing packaged insights for clients seeking actionable intelligence.

Remember, there's no one-size-fits-all solution in the data industry. The optimal packaging strategy is one that best aligns with your company's capabilities, resources, and market understanding. Your early choices will provide the foundation upon which your company is built and will significantly influence its future growth and development.

Vital Task 4: Validate the Data

As a data company, before you can convince potential clients of your data's value proposition, you need to be certain of its fidelity to ground truth.

Ground truth refers to the reality that your data represents or seeks to capture. Validating ground truth involves confirming that your data accurately mirrors the phenomena, patterns, or events it purports to represent. This is an important step, as it provides confidence in the data and forms the basis for any subsequent analysis, modeling, or prediction.

Unlike software companies, data companies face the unique challenge of not only demonstrating the usefulness of their product but also proving its truthfulness. Just as a builder wouldn't start construction on an unstable foundation, a data company cannot begin building its product offerings without first validating its data's quality and reliability.

Validating data is an internal process, a necessary step before tailoring data to specific client needs. It's about ensuring that your data faithfully represents reality from which you can extract valuable, reliable insights.

Case Study: Facteus and the Validation of Ground Truth

Facteus faced the challenge of validating its data's ground truth when it was still in its early stages. Their vast data contained millions of transactions, but was it a faithful representation of consumer behavior? Could it accurately reflect the trends, patterns, and spending habits of the consumer market at large?

Facteus sought to answer these questions by leveraging a trusted and recognized source of public data: the Monthly Retail Sales Report from the U.S. Census Bureau. This report, available at census.gov, provides a comprehensive view of retail sales in the United States, categorized by different spending areas. It serves as a reliable benchmark for consumer spending trends, making it an ideal reference for Facteus.

The Monthly Retail Sales Report splits retail sales into various categories: clothing, electronics, groceries, and fuel spending. Each category is accompanied by monthly sales figures dating back several years, providing a rich dataset for comparison and analysis. This detailed breakdown offered Facteus the opportunity to compare their data with the Census Bureau's data on a category-by-category basis, beginning with major spending categories in their dataset.

Take the fuel category. Fuel spending is a significant part of consumer expenditures, and fluctuations in this spending can indicate broader economic trends. To validate their data in this category, Facteus compared their transaction data—specifically, fuel-related transactions—with the fuel spending figures from the Census Bureau's report. They conducted this analysis month-over-month to capture the dynamic nature of consumer spending.

This involved an analysis to measure the correlation between Facteus' data and the Census Bureau's data. A high correlation value from this analysis would suggest that their data was a reliable representation of the larger spending patterns in the fuel category.

The outcome was positive. The analysis revealed a high correlation value, affirming the accuracy and representativeness of Facteus' data. This was a clear indication that their data accurately mirrored the ground truth of consumer spending behavior in the fuel category.

After validating the fuel category, Facteus repeated this exercise with other major categories within their dataset. The objective was to validate their data across multiple dimensions of consumer spending, providing a comprehensive view of its accuracy and representativeness.

This validation not only enhanced their confidence in the data but also boosted their credibility with potential clients. By demonstrating a strong correlation with a recognized and trusted public dataset, Facteus could prove that its data was a reliable source of consumer transaction information.

Validating the ground truth doesn't directly solve a specific customer need or job. However, it assures customers and the data company itself that the data being used is accurate, representative, and ready to be employed to solve problems, create insights, and drive decisions. This key step served as a foundation upon which Facteus could build its various data offerings, providing assurance to both the company and its potential clients about the quality and accuracy of the data they were working with.

In Review:

- **Data Productization Process:** We explored the transformation of raw, unstructured data into consumable, valuable insights for commercial use, highlighting the importance of structuring and presenting data in an accessible and usable way for customers.

- **'Jobs to Be Done' Framework:** We applied this framework to data products, focusing on identifying customer needs that the data product should fulfill, moving beyond the data's attributes to what it can accomplish for the customer.

- **Data Enhancement:** We augmented data with additional features like Named Entity Recognition (NER), enhancing its value and creating links between different data sets to multiply potential use cases.

- **Packaging Data:** We discussed optimizing data packaging for different clients, industries, and markets, ensuring the data is accessible and user-friendly.

- **Data Validation:** We discussed verifying the representativeness and accuracy of data and determining its fidelity to ground truth, which is essential for building credible and reliable data products.

- **Pricing Strategies:** We explored effective pricing of data products, balancing the art and science of pricing to align with the value offered.

- **Real-World Case Studies:** We included case studies, like the consumer transaction data company Facteus, to demonstrate practical applications of these concepts in enhancing and packaging data for specific market needs.

- **Data Enhancements and Market Expansion:** We emphasized how strategic data enhancements can open up new markets, create new opportunities, and tailor data to meet diverse customer needs, thus expanding the reach and utility of data products.

CHAPTER 3
MARKETING FOR
DATA COMPANIES

MARKETING FOR
DATA COMPANIES

As we've stressed throughout this book, data is unlike any other product or service—and it's definitely not software. It's a unique vertical with its own rules, demands, and potential. As data companies strive to articulate their unique value, stand out from the competition, and establish meaningful connections with their customer base, the need for a data-specific marketing strategy becomes evident. Data companies need an approach that not only highlights the value of their data products but also communicates this value in interesting and relatable ways to the target audience.

In this chapter, we will unpack the complexities of marketing for data companies, exploring key themes and strategies to illuminate the path ahead. We will discuss how data companies can showcase their data, like the iconic Ikea catalog, making it tangible and desirable to potential customers. We will dive into the nuances of positioning your data, demonstrating how to articulate your unique value proposition in a crowded marketplace. We'll explore the critical role of context, or the job your data executes, in shaping your marketing messages.

We will discuss strategies for reaching out to your potential customers and making them aware of the unique solutions your data can offer. Finally, we will explore ways to leverage data marketplaces, emerging platforms that are reshaping how data is bought and sold.

Not All Tech Companies Are Created Equal

Data companies are fundamentally distinct from software or traditional businesses, and this distinction permeates every facet of their operation, including marketing. The uniqueness of a data company starts from the product it offers—data itself or access to unique data. Unlike software or physical products, data is an intangible asset with nuanced value. While the value of a piece of software or a physical product can be relatively straightforward to demonstrate, the value of a dataset is often hidden in correlations, predictive powers, the ability to inform decisions, and information asymmetry. We might even go so far as to say that data companies are all marketing—that is, their success relies on the ability to explain why and how the data is useful rather than just releasing a piece of software and waiting for people to make use of it. This sometimes hard-to-access value necessitates a marketing approach that goes beyond simply showcasing the product; it demands a strategy that highlights the power of data to inform, predict, and enable effective decision-making and information arbitrage.

As we discussed earlier, data markets often favor the provider with the most comprehensive dataset, resulting in a competitive landscape where the large often get larger, and the small struggle to find a footing. This market dynamic needs to be factored into the marketing strategy. A data company's marketing messages must convincingly communicate its capability to provide comprehensive and valuable datasets that can outperform the competition.

Furthermore, data products are not standalone. They derive value from integrating well with the customer's existing systems and processes. This integration-centric value proposition requires a marketing strategy that does more than simply promote the data product. It must highlight how well the data product can be integrated and used within the customer's specific context and industry.

In this way, while file-sharing companies like Dropbox no longer need to explain what file-sharing software is, data companies often need to educate the market. Unlike established product categories where customers are actively searching for solutions, potential customers of data products may not even be aware of the problems that these products can solve. This calls for a marketing approach that is not only promotional but also educational.

Case Study: Showcasing Your Product Like Ikea

When we think about industry disruptors that have brought a groundbreaking approach to their respective sectors, Ikea immediately stands out. Known for their creative and innovative approach, the Swedish multinational giant transformed how we think about furniture—from its design and manufacturing to its packaging and distribution.

Ikea's innovations came to life with their pioneering flat-pack furniture model, which allows for easy transportation and self-assembly. This approach not only disrupted the furniture industry but also presented customers with an empowering and cost-effective solution that didn't compromise style or quality. They streamlined the production process, and their innovative self-service model in stores drove down costs and passed those savings onto customers.

The price component of this proposition is easily quantifiable and can be communicated straightforwardly. However, communicating the design aesthetics and the potential of Ikea's furniture to transform a living space required a different approach.

Imagine a catalog that only included photos of the opened boxes, with all the styrofoam, tools, and bags of accessories. That wouldn't be a great marketing decision. Similarly, hoping to get new customers by marketing how many columns your dataset has or by sharing the innards of your proprietary algorithm is a losing game. You must show them what it looks like when it's all put together and how the time and effort required to set it up will be worth it.

The Ikea catalog, more than a simple listing of products, lets potential customers visualize the furniture in their own homes and the homes they aspire to have. It showcases its products in the context of beautifully designed and decorated living spaces, giving potential customers a vision of what's possible with Ikea's furniture. Much like what your data company's marketing should do, the Ikea catalog provides context and sparks the imagination. Give your potential customers something to dream about rather than throwing down the dataset like some flat-packed furniture and telling them to do their best. Without their sleek, organized, and aspirational marketing and cataloging, Ikea's value proposition is significantly less attractive. Most data companies just lay out all the parts of their furniture and hope someone understands carpentry enough to hobble it together.

How can we showcase our data products in a way that helps our customers see the transformative possibilities? The objective here isn't just to sell data but to stimulate a shift in mindset, inspiring potential customers with the idea of what they could achieve with your data.

The value of data lies not in its raw form but in its potential to inform decisions, yield insights, and drive action. But, like an unassembled Ikea product, this potential is often not immediately apparent. Instead, the potential of data is revealed only when it's organized, analyzed, and applied in a meaningful context.

As a data company, your task is similar to Ikea's: to help customers envision the transformative possibilities that your product offers. It's vital to illustrate the value creation involved in the process of hiring your data to complete their tasks, much in the same way people understand what value they are getting from putting together Ikea furniture. This entails not just marketing the data itself but showcasing how this data can be assembled and utilized to create value. For data companies, assembly might take the form of analysis, integration, and application to specific business problems. This intermediate stage of data assembly will satisfy a broader segment of customers than raw data alone will. If there were no assembly instructions, only carpenters would buy Ikea. Similarly, for customers with data processing capabilities, like the hedge funds we mentioned in Chapter 2, raw data is enough to understand the product's value and make a buying decision. They can appreciate the structure, understand the insights it might reveal, and envision how it could fit into their operations.

The Ikea catalog asks nothing of the viewer except to imagine. It doesn't require the customer to have a working knowledge of furniture assembly or an eye for interior design. Instead, it presents a fully realized vision of the product's potential, offering an accessible and attractive representation of what could be.

Although data isn't as immediately tangible or visually engaging as furniture, there are still ways to communicate its value convincingly. Data companies can showcase their real-world relevance and potential by presenting their data products in context—through dashboards, visualized reports, or correlating them to current events.

By minimizing the cognitive effort required to comprehend the data's potential applications and benefits, data companies can draw in a wider audience. Instead of asking prospective customers to understand abstract data points, they can demonstrate the data's value in a meaningful, relatable context.

Case Study: Facteus and the Ikea Approach

Facteus had the valuable asset of a comprehensive transaction dataset. Their data held a wealth of insights, but they faced a significant challenge when trying to sell to retailers. The issue was that the data, in its raw or somewhat aggregated form, was much like Ikea furniture laid out piece by piece. It took a lot of work for potential customers to envision how they would make use of it.

Though the retailers represented a vast market opportunity for Facteus, they needed considerable assistance to understand the value of transaction data. Like most customers before an unassembled Ikea bookcase, retailers were unsure how to piece together the various elements of raw transaction data into a coherent, meaningful, and useful structure.

Recognizing this barrier to adoption, Facteus built a demo dashboard that allowed retailers to instantly visualize the transaction data in a more comprehensible and applicable manner. This dashboard was far from a fully baked SaaS product. It was a tool that showcased the data like the beautiful, full-page images in an IKEA catalog.

In the dashboard, retailers could interact with the transaction data in a user-friendly and intuitive manner. They could select specific competitors and derive insights into their market shares by region and age demographic. Though the data was incomplete and slightly irrelevant so as not to give away their product for free, it excited potential customers about sifting through the data for their own purposes.

Let's hypothetically consider someone in Nike's marketing department. They could use the Facteus dashboard to understand how Nike's market share stacked up against Adidas, particularly during high-profile global events like the World Cup. By inputting parameters of their interest, such as a specific time period (before, during, and after the World Cup) and regions (countries participating in the World Cup), they could analyze changes in market share and consumer behavior.

Moreover, they could break down these trends by age demographics to see if there were significant shifts among certain age groups. Were millennials more swayed towards Adidas after their World Cup campaign? Did this trend persist over time, or was it just a temporary spike? With this level of detail, the Nike marketer could gain insights into consumer behavior and competitor performance during specific global events.

This level of insight didn't just make the transaction data understandable—it made it actionable. The marketing strategist at Nike, or any other retailer using Facteus' data, could immediately see the relevance of the transaction data to their operations and strategic planning. The dashboard allowed them to not just view the data but interact with it, draw out trends, make comparisons, and understand their position in the market in a far more nuanced manner.

The demo dashboard allowed Facteus to overcome the understanding gap that had been a significant hurdle in their marketing efforts. The results were transformative. After introducing the demo dashboard, Facteus saw a significant upturn in its growth curve. Their approach had turned an abstract concept—transaction data—into a tangible and valuable tool. It allowed Facteus to break into the retail market for transaction data, paving the way for its rapid expansion. The lesson was clear: adopting an IKEA catalog-style approach to showcasing their data product is a winning strategy.

Competing Against Giants

A key strategic element for data companies is to determine how to position their data offerings. While the nature of data might be considered ubiquitous and universal, the way it's packaged, delivered, and presented can differ greatly. Your company's data products need to carve out their own unique space in the market, demonstrating a value proposition that distinguishes them from competitors.

This concept of positioning is particularly crucial given the 'winner takes most' dynamics observed in data markets. In a marketplace saturated with data options, how can your data shine as the standout choice that delivers value to users? How can you compete with giants who have been excelling in the data game for years or decades This section will explore how to leverage the 'winner takes most' dynamic to your advantage by navigating the delicate balance between blending into the data landscape and standing out as a unique, indispensable resource.

Positioning is about identifying a niche in the market where your data product can become the leading choice. It's about finding an intersection of your data's unique strengths, your technical competencies, and a significant customer need. Successful positioning allows your data product to be recognized as a leading choice in a particular segment, standing out amongst competitors.

Similarly, defining your data's 'job' is clearly expressing the primary problem your data solves for customers. This step elucidates your data's value proposition, giving prospective customers an immediate grasp of your product's benefits. It paints a picture of how your data fits into and enhances their current processes or objectives.

Carving out a niche and defining a 'job' for your data doesn't guarantee success on its own. The chosen niche must be substantial enough to support a robust business case. This consideration brings us back to the 'winner takes most' dynamic that is common in the data industry.

Given this dynamic, your niche should be broad enough to attract a significant customer base yet specialized enough to allow your data product to demonstrate clear superiority. For instance, if your data provides deep, real-time insights into consumer behavior, you might position your product as the preferred choice for businesses looking to optimize marketing strategies. Here, the 'job' of your data could be to empower companies to craft highly targeted, data-driven marketing campaigns.

In a highly competitive and crowded market, merely having a valuable data product doesn't cut it. You need to strategically position your product and articulate its 'job,' ensuring the market segment you focus on is large enough to sustain your business in a 'winner takes most' industry. Balancing these considerations is critical to positioning your data company for success.

Misconceptions: Directive vs. Dreamscape

Software companies, with their predetermined and defined value propositions, can craft a straightforward narrative for their marketing. They provide solutions to distinct problems, and their marketing message is typically straightforward: "Our software solves this particular problem or fulfills this specific need." This clarity facilitates the creation of persuasive marketing content. A software company can easily articulate its product's features, benefits, and unique selling points and align them with the identified needs or challenges of its target audience.

On the other hand, marketing for data companies is akin to selling a Swiss army knife. The value of the data is not finite; it is versatile, adaptable, and capable of serving a broad range of use cases. Therefore, the marketing message cannot be confined to specific features or solutions. Instead, it needs to illustrate the vast array of possibilities that the data can offer while also sparking the imagination of potential customers, prompting them to visualize the numerous ways they can utilize the data to address their unique needs or questions. The buyer needs to understand how much more prepared they will be with this Swiss Army knife in their pocket.

This is the fine line that data companies must tread. They need to highlight specific use cases to show the tangible value their data can provide. Yet, they must also communicate the breadth and depth of possibilities their data can offer.

This nuanced marketing strategy demands an in-depth understanding of the customer's business, the ability to speak their language, and the creativity to both illustrate specific applications and inspire broader exploration. It differs significantly from the more focused, problem-solving approach of software companies, and mastering this art of marketing vast possibilities is not just important but vital to a data company's success.

Understanding these nuances is not just about dispelling misconceptions; it's about equipping data companies to develop effective marketing strategies that resonate with their unique value proposition and their customers' diverse needs. In the world of data, marketing is about selling potential, the promise of exploration, and the thrill of discovery.

GOOGLE MAPS VS EVERYONE ELSE

In the world of geographic data, there exists an interesting and invaluable segment known as Point of Interest (POI) data. This kind of data pertains to specific geographic locations where someone might find a particular utility or interest. These points could range from restaurants and retail outlets to parks, museums, hospitals, and myriad other destinations. Essentially, POI data gives digital life to the physical world around us.

In our day-to-day lives, we interact with POI data more often than we might realize. When we use navigation software to find a route to a nearby cafe, when we use apps like OpenTable to book a restaurant reservation, or when we explore a new city using a tour guide app, we're engaging with POI data.

The landscape of the POI data industry seems to be dominated by one player—Google. Its service, Google Maps, has revolutionized how we understand and navigate our surroundings. With an extensive database of locations and an easy-to-use interface, Google Maps stands as a towering presence in the POI data space.

Yet, the landscape isn't as one-sided as it may appear. There are several data-as-a-service providers who successfully compete against this tech giant, illustrating the potential for differentiation and successful positioning in the data market, even when faced with a seemingly invincible competitor.

In this section, we will tackle the complex journeys of these successful niche players in the POI data space, their strategies, and the distinct 'job' they've defined for their data. These stories offer valuable insights into effective marketing and positioning for data companies, showing how it's possible to compete and win against even the most formidable opponents.

CASE STUDY: FOURSQUARE

Against the backdrop of the Google-dominated landscape, Foursquare has carved out a successful niche for itself in the Point of Interest (POI) data industry. Initially launched as a social networking service where users could 'check-in' at different locations and share their whereabouts with friends, Foursquare has since pivoted to become a leading provider of location data and technology.

A primary strength of Foursquare's offering lies in the rich detail and accuracy of its data. Its API provides access to an extensive database of over 105 million global points of interest, which is significantly more than many competitors. But it's not just the quantity of data that sets Foursquare apart—it's the quality. Foursquare's data is enriched with user-generated content, such as check-ins, tips, ratings, and photos. This user engagement lends a distinct depth to the data, providing valuable context and richness beyond a location's simple geographic coordinates.

Foursquare has also differentiated itself through its unique 'visit' data. While Google Maps excels at showcasing popular times for a location, Foursquare takes it a step further. Its technology can detect when users visit physical locations, and this anonymous visit data can provide unique insights into consumer behavior patterns. This extra layer of detailed, context-rich information helps Foursquare stand out.

Foursquare has positioned itself as the go-to source for businesses that need more than just basic POI data. They cater to companies seeking a deeper understanding of consumer behaviors and location dynamics. Their data enables businesses to personalize customer experiences, make more informed location-based decisions, and ultimately gain a competitive edge.

One example of a Foursquare business customer is Redfin, a modern real estate platform. Redfin realized that its users needed more than just details about properties. They were also interested in what a neighborhood had to offer—from its restaurants and parks to shopping centers and schools.

Here's where Foursquare's detailed POI data entered the picture. Instead of using Google, Redfin turned to Foursquare's Places database to provide this much-needed neighborhood context. By integrating Foursquare's data, Redfin was able to offer users detailed, accurate, and up-to-date information about the businesses and services surrounding the properties listed on their platform.

If a user was looking at a home listing in New York, Redfin, powered by Foursquare's data, could display nearby points of interest. This could include the trendy café around the corner, the well-reviewed bakery down the street, or the local farmer's market that operates on weekends. This information helps potential buyers understand the area's ambiance and lifestyle, contributing significantly to their decision-making process.

Foursquare's rich data gave Redfin's listings an edge over its competitors. Not only did the data enhance the value of the listings themselves, but it also enhanced the user experience by providing a holistic view of what living in a particular area would be like. This gave Redfin a competitive advantage, providing them with a more complete and appealing experience to home buyers searching for real estate.

Redfin's partnership with Foursquare showcases the potential of well-positioned data. Foursquare understood the 'job' its data was performing and marketed its advantage of having context-rich data over Google's more generic offerings. By doing so, it was able to win business from a company that required more than just the basics, demonstrating the potential success when data companies clearly define and communicate the unique value they bring to the table.

Despite operating in a market dominated by Google, Foursquare's achievements highlight the importance of meticulous market positioning and clearly defining the distinctive role their data plays. Their journey is a testament to the fact that there is always an opportunity to stand out and offer unparalleled value, even in a saturated marketplace.

This is an example of the 'Jobs to be Done' framework we explored earlier. Foursquare positioned itself beautifully to explain to companies that their unique offerings would superpower companies like Redfin and elevate them far above simply showing the property on an embedded Google Map.

Importantly, Foursquare's success doesn't lie in trying to outmatch Google on every front. Instead, it thrived by carefully selecting the battlefields on which it could excel. By carving out a specific niche and focusing on areas where it can outperform the competition, Foursquare has been able to communicate a unique value proposition to its customers. Foursquare realized that while it would lose the battle with Google for the largest number of users and biggest dataset, it could win the battle for the deepest dataset and most valuable data points for locations. This careful and thoughtful approach to positioning has played a significant role in Foursquare's success, offering valuable lessons to other data companies in a similar position.

MARKETING MESSAGING: ADDRESSING NEEDS, NOT DATA

In the world of data, it's easy to become absorbed in the granular details—the intricacies and complexities of the datasets themselves. But imagine if a car mechanic focused on selling you spark plugs, fuel injectors, or timing belts rather than the promise of a smoothly functioning vehicle. This analogy illuminates a common pitfall when it comes to effective marketing messaging for data companies: a focus on the parts rather than the whole.

Most potential customers are not in the market for data itself but rather the insights, solutions, and answers that data can provide. They're looking for the "smoothly running car," not the individual components under the hood. Just as you wouldn't search for a timing belt when you want a reliable ride to work, customers aren't looking for raw data when they're seeking insight into consumer trends, market shifts, or competitive analysis.

When crafting their marketing messages, data companies must remember this principle. It's not about the nuts and bolts—it's about the journey they enable and the destination they help reach.

Take the case of Facteus and its transaction data. Few people would spontaneously begin a search for a "consumer transaction data set" when trying to uncover market trends or shopper behavior. Instead, they will likely search for more specific, problem-oriented queries like "shifts in consumer shopping habits" or "which streaming service added the most subscribers in the fall?"

When we refer to 'search' in this context, it isn't limited to literal web or search engine queries. It's a broader concept that relates to how people think when trying to solve problems or satisfy needs. People think in terms of the outcomes they desire or the problems they need to solve rather than the tools (in this case, data) that might help them get there.

This is an important aspect for data companies to consider when crafting marketing messages. Instead of primarily focusing on their data's features or attributes, their messaging should concentrate on the problems their data can help solve, the needs it can satisfy, or the goals it can help achieve.

By matching their messaging to these queries and needs, data companies can connect more directly with their potential customers. They can demonstrate the value of their data not as an abstract concept but as a practical solution to real-world challenges, providing the insights and answers they seek.

Data Marketplaces: An Emerging Paradigm or Premature Proposition?

Marketplaces have long served as the backbone of trade and commerce. Traditionally, they were physical spaces, such as open-air markets, bazaars, or shopping centers, where buyers and sellers convene to exchange goods and services. However, in our modern digital age, this concept has evolved to take on new dimensions. Today's marketplaces are digital platforms that bridge geographical distances, time zones, and cultural divides, connecting buyers and sellers across the globe with unprecedented efficiency.

Tech companies like eBay, Uber, Lyft, and Airbnb exemplify this digital marketplace model. eBay serves as a virtual bazaar where people can sell everything from vintage clothes to rare collectibles, connecting sellers to potential buyers across the world. Meanwhile, Uber and Lyft act as intermediaries between drivers and riders, dynamically connecting those who offer a service with those who need it. Airbnb does the same for homeowners and travelers, connecting those with space to spare and those needing a place to stay.

At their core, these marketplaces solve a critical problem: efficiently connecting buyers and sellers at scale. Without these platforms, finding and connecting with a suitable counterparty among the ocean of potential buyers or sellers would be time-consuming and highly inefficient. By centralizing the exchange on a single platform, these marketplaces streamline the process, saving users time and effort while offering a broader range of options than would otherwise be feasible.

The value that these marketplaces bring extends beyond simplifying connections. They also help establish trust through rating and review systems, promote transparency with clear pricing models, and offer transaction support and safeguards.

As we contemplate the idea of integrating these marketplace principles into the world of data, it's critical to approach this notion with a level of discernment. While data is frequently analogized as the new oil, we must be aware that the data industry is still maturing and evolving. It has yet to reach the immense scale of the retail or service industries where the marketplace model thrives, such as those for products like eBay or services like Uber and Airbnb. Data marketplaces, aiming to efficiently connect data buyers and sellers, could undeniably simplify the data buying process and unlock numerous opportunities for innovation and insights. Nevertheless, the readiness to adopt this model and the timing of its deployment in an industry that is still growing and defining itself are subjects worthy of further exploration.

THE CHALLENGES OF DATA MARKETPLACES: DECODING CONTEXTUAL APPLICATIONS

To grasp the obstacles a data marketplace faces, we must circle back to our previous discussion on marketing messaging. Recall that potential customers, particularly those in the early stages of data adoption, rarely search for 'data' itself. Instead, they look for solutions to specific problems or trends that can inform their strategic decisions.

In a typical marketplace like eBay, buyers enter with a specific product in mind. They understand what they're looking for and how it serves their needs. In contrast, a data marketplace must contend with buyers who are often seeking solutions to questions like, "Which streaming service gained the most subscribers last fall?" or "What are the emerging consumer spending trends?"

Thus, a data marketplace has a far more complex task than simply listing available datasets. The marketplace needs to understand the potential applications and contexts of every dataset that is listed. It must interpret a buyer's need and correctly map it to the right data product. That's no easy feat considering the abstract nature of data, its myriad use cases, and the potential for multiple interpretations based on the user's perspective.

A major hurdle a data marketplace must tackle is avoiding the pitfall of becoming just another data catalog. Without the proper context or relevance, a data marketplace runs the risk of presenting a deluge of datasets to potential buyers, potentially resulting in an information overload. This can be daunting and may create a barrier to entry, particularly for those new to data buying.

When a data marketplace merely lists available datasets, it places the onus on the potential buyer to sift through vast amounts of information, discerning the value and applicability of each dataset to their specific needs. This is not a trivial task. Data is inherently abstract, with its value deeply tied to specific use cases, contexts, and interpretations. Given these complexities, the probability of successful matchmaking between data sets and customer queries in a catalog-style marketplace is, unfortunately, low.

The issue is further exacerbated when you consider the diverse needs and levels of data literacy among potential buyers. Some may struggle to articulate their requirements or to understand which data might be most beneficial to them. Others may feel overwhelmed by the array of choices and abandon their search due to the perceived complexity.

Ultimately, by operating as a simple catalog, a data marketplace may inadvertently turn away potential customers by overwhelming them with too many choices or failing to demonstrate the relevance and value of the listed data products to their specific needs. The lesson here is clear: context, relevance, and tailored messaging are critical in data marketplaces. Perfecting these areas remains a substantial challenge that the industry is still grappling with, offering considerable scope for innovation and improvement.

The role of a data marketplace, then, goes beyond merely connecting buyers and sellers. It must play a pivotal role in educating the market, translating data into insights, and demonstrating how those insights can address specific business problems or opportunities. This requires a deep understanding of both the data on offer and the diverse needs of potential buyers. It's an exciting but formidable challenge that has yet to be fully met in the data industry.

THE CHALLENGES OF CONTEXTUALIZING DIVERSE DATA TYPES FOR MARKETPLACES

In a data marketplace, the task of connecting buyers to the data they need becomes a considerable challenge when one considers the sheer variety and complexity of data types. Transaction data, which we discussed earlier, is just the tip of the iceberg. In addition to financial transactions, there are myriad other types of data, such as satellite imagery, social media sentiment, web traffic statistics, geospatial data, IoT sensor data, and much more, all with unique contexts and potential applications.

For instance, satellite data may be utilized in a range of fields, from tracking climate change and assisting disaster response to enhancing precision agriculture. Social media sentiment data can provide valuable insights for brand management, public relations, product development, and political campaigns. Similarly, web traffic data can play a vital role in digital marketing, competitive analysis, user experience design, and SEO strategies.

Each data type is as distinct as the next, with unique features, strengths, and applications. It is critical to understand the context of each data type—the who, what, where, when, why, and how of its generation and potential use. It's not enough for a data marketplace to merely facilitate the exchange of these diverse datasets. For a data marketplace to truly serve its users, it needs to provide a nuanced understanding of these varied data types, their potential uses, and how they can address the specific needs of buyers.

This is easier said than done. Contextualizing and understanding the applications of all these diverse data types demands a profound knowledge of various industries, the latest trends, and potential use cases. This goes beyond the purview of a simple search algorithm or a cataloging system. It requires an amalgamation of deep domain expertise, sophisticated AI algorithms, and, perhaps most importantly, an understanding of the buyers' needs and the problems they are looking to solve.

The challenge for a data marketplace is not only about housing diverse datasets but also about interpreting and communicating the value and relevance of each dataset to its potential users. It's about transforming raw, abstract data into actionable insights and solutions, a task that requires innovation and breakthroughs in both technology and approach.

EVALUATING THE NEED FOR DATA MARKETPLACES: IS IT TOO EARLY?

Given the current landscape of the Data-as-a-Service (DaaS) industry, we must consider whether the industry is indeed ready for a dedicated data marketplace. At present, thousands of datasets are available in the DaaS industry. However, only a handful of providers consistently deliver high-quality data products that bring substantial value to their clients.

In traditional marketplaces like eBay, Amazon, or even Airbnb, the effectiveness and value of the platform are directly tied to the volume and variety of the inventory it houses. A marketplace thrives when it can offer an expansive array of options, catering to diverse needs, preferences, and price points. The wide selection not only attracts a larger number of buyers but also facilitates competition, which can lead to better quality offerings and more competitive pricing.

In the context of the DaaS industry, the relatively small number of high-quality datasets could pose a challenge to the creation of a thriving data marketplace. With limited inventory, the marketplace may struggle to provide the breadth and depth of data offerings necessary to attract and serve a wide array of data buyers. This scenario could also limit the competitive dynamics that drive innovation and improvement in marketplace offerings.

Furthermore, the diversity of data types and use cases adds another layer of complexity to this challenge. As discussed in the previous section, understanding and matching these diverse data types to specific buyer needs is a formidable task requiring an advanced level of sophistication and domain knowledge.

Given the current state of the DaaS industry, it might be premature to establish a dedicated data marketplace. While the concept holds immense potential, the industry might need more maturation, growth, and diversification before a marketplace can truly thrive. Nonetheless, this does not undermine the importance of the goal: creating a platform that efficiently and effectively connects data buyers with high-quality, relevant data offerings. As the DaaS industry continues to evolve and grow, this vision remains a vital goal, shaping the future of data commerce.

In Review:

- **Unique Challenges of Data Company Marketing:** We detailed the distinct challenges faced by data companies in marketing their products, underlining that data, unlike software or physical products, requires a different marketing approach due to its intangible and nuanced nature.

- **Context in Marketing:** We emphasized the critical role of context, or the job the data performs, in shaping marketing messages, highlighting the need for data companies to focus on how their data can be integrated and utilized within the customer's specific industry and systems.

- **Educational Aspect of Marketing:** We explored the necessity for data companies to educate the market, as potential customers may not be actively seeking data products or may not understand their potential applications.

- **Showcasing Data Products Effectively:** We discussed strategies for showcasing data products in a convincing manner, akin to the Ikea catalog, making data tangible and desirable by providing context and sparking the imagination of potential customers.

- **Facteus Case Study:** We examined how Facteus, a consumer transaction data company, successfully used a demo dashboard to make their data product more comprehensible and applicable to retailers, thereby overcoming barriers to adoption.

- **Competing Against Established Players:** We analyzed strategies for competing in data markets dominated by large players, focusing on the importance of positioning data offerings uniquely and defining the distinct 'job' of the data.

- **Differentiating Data Marketing from Software Marketing:** We contrasted data marketing with software marketing, noting that data marketing needs to highlight a broad range of possibilities and inspire exploration rather than focusing solely on specific features or solutions.

- **Challenges and Potential of Data Marketplaces:** We assessed the challenges and potential of developing data marketplaces, recognizing the complexities involved in connecting buyers with relevant data products and the current maturity level of the Data-as-a-Service industry.

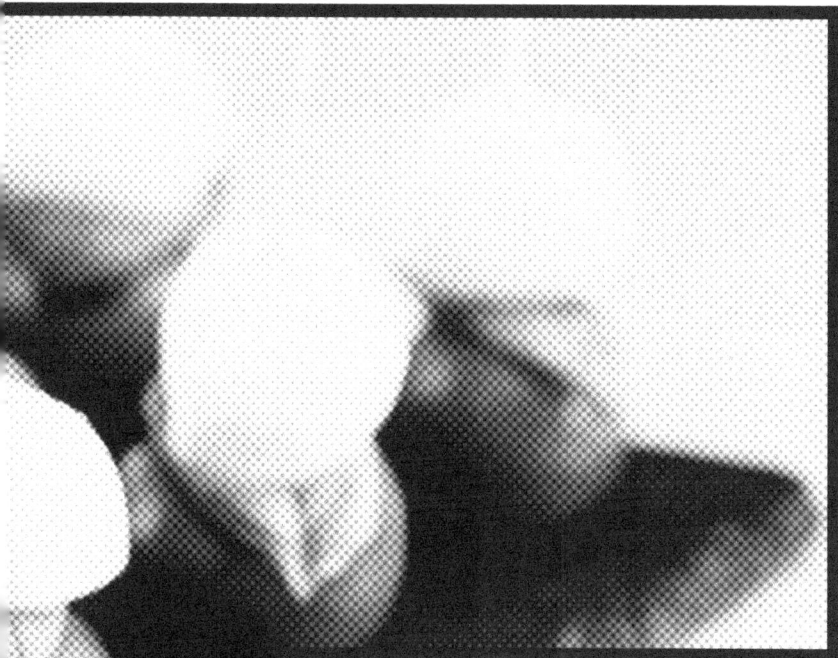

CHAPTER 4
MASTERING THE CRAFT
OF DATA SALES

MASTERING THE CRAFT
OF DATA SALES

When selling software, the playbook often involves demonstrating sleek interfaces, showing off a roster of impressive features, and illustrating immediate functional benefits. But the story takes an exciting twist when it comes to selling data. Here, your task is to create a vivid narrative around the untapped potential that the data embodies: the prospective insights, the informed decisions it could drive, and the latent value waiting to be unlocked. It demands an intimate understanding of the data in your arsenal, along with a deep insight into your customer's pain points and aspirations.

This chapter unfolds a narrative that might seem unorthodox to traditional salespeople, especially those honed in selling software or services. Yet, it's precisely this nonconformity that makes the sales process for data so fascinating and rewarding. Unlike most sales pipelines, a critical aspect of the DaaS (Data-as-a-service) pipeline is evaluation and testing. Much like a potential car buyer insists on a test drive before closing the deal, a prospective data buyer will invariably want to assess the data's quality, relevance, and potential to deliver the promised insights. How you facilitate this 'test drive,' managing expectations while highlighting your data's strength—and without handing them over all the data—forms a key aspect of the data sales process that we will examine in this chapter.

This chapter will equip you with the strategies, tools, and mindset to successfully navigate the complexities of data sales. Through a blend of theory, practical challenges, real-world case studies, and proven strategies, we'll provide a comprehensive understanding of selling in the data landscape.

Crafting the Perfect Data Sample

Selling data involves many complexities. One of the most notable is generating data samples for potential customers, akin to handing out food samples at a bustling Costco. The objective is to entice the customers' taste buds just enough to make them want more, but not so much that they walk away completely satisfied and sated with the sample alone. There are five key elements to crafting the perfect data sample.

SHOWCASING VALUE WITHOUT OVERSHARING

The sample must be a genuine representation of the data product's quality, relevance, and potential value. It needs to be substantial enough to allow the customer to run real tests and see genuine insights but limited enough not to fulfill their entire need.

Example: A data provider specializing in retail trends offers a sample that includes data from a single region over a one-week period. The sample illustrates clear trends and actionable insights, but it's limited in scope. Clients can see how the data might benefit them, but they will need the full dataset to conduct a comprehensive analysis across all regions and timeframes.

UNDERSTANDING CUSTOMER NEEDS

Crafting the perfect data sample requires a deep understanding of what the customer is looking to achieve. What are their pain points? What insights are they seeking? The sample must be tailored to demonstrate how your data can provide solutions to these specific issues. Generic or misaligned samples can lead to misunderstandings and missed opportunities.

Example: A healthcare data company tailors a sample specifically for a research institute studying diabetes. The sample includes data directly related to risk factors for diabetes and patient outcomes but omits unrelated health data. This alignment with the institute's specific goals makes the sample more relevant and cogent.

PROTECTING INTELLECTUAL PROPERTY

While your samples must be generous, they must also safeguard against the potential risk of giving away too much. It's about striking the right balance between providing a taste of the product and protecting the intellectual property inherent in your data. Ensuring that the sample does not dilute the core value proposition of the entire dataset is vital.

Example: A company offering social media sentiment analysis provides a sample that shows the trends and overall sentiment towards a particular product but doesn't give away the proprietary algorithms and detailed breakdowns that form the core of their offering. This maintains intrigue and protects intellectual property.

SETTING CLEAR BOUNDARIES AND EXPECTATIONS

A well-defined data sample is accompanied by clear communication regarding its scope, limitations, and intended use. This ensures that the customer knows exactly what they are getting and avoids any misunderstandings that might arise from perceived discrepancies between the sample and the final product.

Example: A provider of financial market data offers a free sample with an explicit agreement stating the sample's limitations, such as being only for evaluation purposes and not for commercial use. This ensures that the client understands the terms of the trial, fostering transparent communication.

Providing a sample is not a 'set and forget' action. It's part of a dynamic and interactive process where the customer may need guidance on how to interpret or apply the data. The ongoing support, dialogue, and engagement during the evaluation period can make a profound difference in building trust and closing the sale.

Example: A weather data company provides a sample to a logistics firm and pairs it with continuous support from a dedicated data specialist. The specialist helps the logistics firm understand how to integrate the weather data into their route planning, enhancing the value of the sample and building a rapport that facilitates the sales process.

Case Study: Facteus and the Perfect Data Sample for a Large National Coffee Shop Chain

Facteus, a leading provider of consumer transaction data, had a unique opportunity to showcase the value of its data to a large national coffee shop chain. This well-known chain was grappling with a pressing concern: the rise of local, high-end artisanal coffee shops and their impact on the chain's market share across the country. To address this challenge, the coffee chain needed to ensure that Facteus' data was the right fit and could provide the insights it needed to understand and respond to this market shift.

Facteus recognized that crafting the perfect data sample was pivotal to winning the coffee chain's business. They needed to demonstrate the value of their data while protecting their intellectual property and ensuring that the sample was tailored to the chain's specific needs. The Facteus team understood that a generic or misaligned sample could lead to missed opportunities and a failure to showcase the true potential of their data.

To create the ideal sample, Facteus chose to focus on a single urban area: San Francisco. This targeted approach allowed them to provide a comprehensive and relevant dataset that directly addressed the coffee chain's concerns. By narrowing the geographic scope, Facteus could offer a more detailed and granular view of the market dynamics in a key location where artisanal coffee shops were thriving.

Moreover, Facteus included multiple years of historical data in the sample. This addition was important, as it enabled the coffee chain to analyze the rise and impact of artisanal coffee chains on their local market share over time. By providing a longitudinal view, Facteus demonstrated the depth and richness of their data, showcasing how it could be used to identify trends, track market changes, and inform strategic decisions.

The San Francisco data sample was carefully curated to strike the right balance between offering valuable insights and protecting Facteus' intellectual property. It provided enough information to demonstrate the data's potential without giving away the full extent of Facteus' capabilities. This approach allowed the coffee chain to run real tests and see genuine insights while leaving room for further exploration and analysis of the entire dataset.

Facteus' thoughtful and targeted approach to crafting the data sample paid off. The sample successfully showcased the value of their data and its relevance to the coffee chain's specific needs. It provided a clear and convincing demonstration of how Facteus' data could help the chain understand and respond to the challenge posed by artisanal coffee shops.

Impressed by the insights gleaned from the San Francisco sample, the national coffee shop chain recognized the potential of Facteus' data to inform its strategy across all major metro areas in the US. The success of the sample led to a larger data deal, with the chain acquiring access to Facteus' full dataset to conduct a comprehensive analysis of the impact of artisanal coffee shops on their market share nationwide.

The Facteus case study highlights the importance of crafting the perfect data sample in the sales process. By understanding the customer's needs, focusing on a specific and relevant geographic area, providing historical data, and striking the right balance between value and protection, Facteus was able to create a sample that effectively demonstrated the power of its data. This tailored approach not only won the coffee chain's business but also laid the foundation for a long-term partnership based on trust and the proven value of Facteus' data.

Misconceptions: Frameworks vs. Creativity

For software companies, the sales process follows a very structured protocol. The value proposition of the software is deterministic and finite, with a clear definition of what the software can and cannot offer. Sales representatives can guide prospects along a well-trodden path, showcasing the features and benefits of their product and linking those benefits to the prospects' specific needs. Usually, pricing also follows a clear structure based on factors such as the number of users, levels of functionality, or the scale of deployment. This straightforward approach allows software companies to standardize their sales process, making it easier to train sales teams and scale their operations. The predictability of the software sales process also makes it easier to forecast revenue and plan for growth.

Picture this process as building a house with a well-defined blueprint. Like an architect, the software company presents the blueprint (the software's capabilities) to the prospective customer (the homeowner), who decides if it's the house they want. There's little room for ambiguity, as the blueprint clearly outlines what the final product will look like. This analogy highlights the predictability and transparency of the software sales process, where customers know exactly what they're getting before they make a purchase. The blueprint also serves as a clear roadmap for the software development team, ensuring they deliver a product meeting the specified requirements.

In stark contrast, the sales process of a data company takes a more creative, solutions-oriented approach. Given that data can be molded to fit a multitude of use cases, the sales team must first understand the prospect's unique needs, challenges, and objectives. This requires a more consultative approach, where the sales team works closely with the prospect to identify opportunities for data-driven solutions. The sales process for data companies is less transactional and more relationship-based, as the sales team needs to build trust and credibility with the prospect to fully understand their business and data needs.

The data sales process is less about demonstrating predefined features and more about helping the prospect envision the potential of the data. The sales team acts more like consultants, collaborating with prospects to tailor a solution that extracts the most value from the data. The pricing, too, often requires a more nuanced approach, reflecting the custom nature of the solution and the unique value it provides. In short, the data company sales process is more exploratory and collaborative than the software sales process. This approach allows data companies to differentiate themselves based on their ability to solve complex problems and deliver unique insights rather than simply competing on price or features. It also enables data companies to build deeper, more strategic relationships with their customers as they become trusted partners in driving business value through data.

This more creative and consultative approach requires a unique type of sales organization—one that can support advanced, technical, and open-minded sales. The sales team needs to be equipped not only with a deep understanding of the data products and domain knowledge of the data but also with the ability to comprehend complex customer needs, work through technical nuances, and design tailored solutions. This goes beyond the traditional sales skills, blending in elements of consulting, data science, and project management. Grasping nuances like this is more than just an intellectual exercise; it's a fundamental prerequisite to unlocking the true potential of data companies and driving their success.

The Balance Between Transparency and Salesmanship

Data sales is a unique landscape where the lines between salesmanship and transparency must be drawn carefully. While other industries, like software, can sell futures (i.e., promising features to be developed later), the data world cannot accommodate such latitude. For a software company, it's possible to promise a feature that will be developed six months down the line.

However, consider the challenge of supplying data as if it were a tangible product. For instance, offering to fabricate data when a client requests information on Gen-X spending behavior would raise concerns regarding the integrity and trustworthiness of the data. It also undermines the very purpose of data-driven decision-making, which relies on authentic and accurate insights to inform strategies and actions. It's both unethical and impossible.

In the domain of data, what you see must indeed be what you get. Data is a tangible product, unyielding in its composition. If your dataset leans heavily toward understanding millennials and Gen-Z, it doesn't possess any hidden insights on Gen-X. That's an innate characteristic of the dataset. Once a client accesses the data, any discrepancies, gaps, or biases become immediately evident. The dance of selling data is a sophisticated one. Instead of concealing what the data might lack, sales efforts should be channeled into emphasizing areas where the data truly shines. This spotlight can be shined in four distinct ways:

HIGHLIGHTING STRENGTHS:

If your data provides unparalleled insights into the online shopping habits of Gen-Z, that's a value proposition. Let's say your dataset reveals that 70% of Gen-Z shoppers make purchasing decisions based on social media influencer recommendations. A brand looking to penetrate the Gen-Z market could leverage this insight to fine-tune its influencer marketing strategy. Focus on clients such as e-commerce platforms or emerging fashion brands targeting younger demographics, for whom such detailed insight would be invaluable.

BEING CANDID:

Transparency isn't just about ethics; it's also good business. If a client's needs genuinely misalign with what your data offers, acknowledge it. Overpromising and under-delivering can tarnish your reputation in the long run.

If a pharmaceutical company approaches you seeking data insights on elderly patients' drug interactions, but your dataset is primarily centered on young adults' wellness habits, it's important to be upfront about the discrepancy between their needs and your offerings. Rather than vaguely promising insights, it's wiser to clearly state the dataset's focus, potentially saving both parties time and resources. Don't sacrifice your ethics for the potential of a deal. In a world saturated with information, trust is the most valuable currency.

FRAMING THE NARRATIVE:

Every dataset has a story. Maybe yours is about understanding the pulse of younger generations. Frame your sales narrative around this, offering clients a lens into a demographic that's shaping the future.

Position your dataset as a 'Gen-Z Pulse Monitor' that tracks not only buying patterns but also emerging trends, cultural shifts, and digital behaviors unique to this age group. By narrating a clear story, a music streaming service might be keen to understand which genres or artists are trending among Gen-Z, allowing them to curate their playlists accordingly.

UNDERSTANDING YOUR VALUE:

 Understanding your data's distinct qualities and advantages is critical to identifying your niche in the market. Rather than pursuing every potential client, it is essential to focus on building robust relationships with those who can genuinely benefit from your offerings.

For instance, consider a scenario where your data company specializes in monitoring the organic food consumption habits of millennials. Instead of pitching to a wide-ranging fast-food chain, direct your efforts towards organic food producers or health-focused startups. These entities are more likely to recognize the value of your data, fostering a more meaningful and enduring partnership. By proactively targeting clients aligned with your data's strengths, you can establish mutually beneficial relationships and maximize the impact of your offerings in the marketplace.

Bridging the Technical Gap in Data Sales

In data sales, the complexity and depth of data products often create a significant technical barrier between the sales team and potential clients. Unlike traditional software or hardware sales, where the features and benefits are more tangible, easily understood, and documented, data products require a deeper level of technical understanding to effectively communicate their value and potential applications.

This is where the role of sales engineers or product support becomes key. These individuals serve as the essential bridge between the intricate world of data and the specific needs and challenges of the client. They possess a unique blend of technical expertise and sales acumen that allows them to translate the complex capabilities of the data product into clear, convincing value propositions tailored to each client's unique requirements.

Sales engineers are the unsung heroes of the data sales process. They dive deep into the client's world, seeking to understand not only their stated objectives but also their underlying pain points and future aspirations. They explore the client's current data analytics and insights approach, identifying gaps and opportunities where the data product can make a significant impact.

Armed with this deep understanding of the client's needs, sales engineers work closely with the product team to tailor the data offering to the client's specific use case. This involves curating and customizing the data to highlight the most relevant insights and features that align with the client's goals. By presenting the data product in the context of the client's unique challenges and opportunities, sales engineers can effectively demonstrate its tangible value and potential for driving business success.

But the role of sales engineers extends far beyond the initial sale. They are the ones who continue to provide ongoing support and guidance to the client, ensuring the successful implementation and adoption of the data product. They are the troubleshooters and problem-solvers, always ready to answer technical questions, assist with data integration, and help the client navigate any challenges that may arise.

In essence, sales engineers are the vital link between the data product and the client. They are the ones who make the complex accessible, the abstract tangible, and the potential realized. Without their expertise and dedication, the true value of data products would remain untapped, and the gap between data and decision-making would remain unbridged.

Sales engineers play four critical roles in the sales process:

UNDERSTANDING THE CLIENT'S USE CASE:

Sales engineers are central to understanding the client's unique use case. They go beyond surface-level objectives and dive deep into the client's specific challenges, goals, and current approach to managing and interpreting data. This thorough understanding is the foundation for the entire sales process.

Example: If a client is a financial analyst looking to forecast consumer spending trends, the sales engineer could investigate the analyst's current forecasting models, data sources, and specific consumer segments of interest. This information helps tailor the consumer spending data to the client's exact requirements. By probing, the sales engineer can gain a comprehensive understanding of the client's needs. They can identify gaps in the client's current approach and pinpoint areas where the data product can provide the most value. This deep understanding allows the sales engineer to tailor the data product to the client's exact requirements, making the offering more powerful and relevant.

TAILORING THE DATA PRODUCT:

Once the sales engineer has a deep understanding of the client's use case, they collaborate with the product team to tailor the data product to the client's specific needs. This involves curating and customizing the data to highlight the most relevant insights and features that align with the client's goals.

Example: If the financial analyst is focused on forecasting spending trends for Gen-Z consumers, the sales engineer could work with the product team to curate a data product that specifically highlights their spending patterns across different industries or product categories. This might involve aggregating the data in a particular way, creating specific data views, or even conducting preliminary analyses to surface key insights. The goal is to present the data in the most meaningful and actionable way for the client. By tailoring the data product to the client's unique needs, the sales engineer can demonstrate the tangible value of the offering and make a strong case for its adoption.

DEMOING THE DATA PRODUCT:

The demo is a critical moment in the sales process, often led by the sales engineer. This is where the sales engineer showcases the data product to the client, highlighting its key features and demonstrating how it aligns with the client's use case.

Example: In the demo, the sales engineer could walk the financial analyst through the consumer spending data, showing how it can help track Gen-Z spending patterns, how it can be integrated into their forecasting models, and how it can enhance the accuracy of their forecasts. The sales engineer might highlight specific trends or patterns in the data, demonstrating how these insights can inform the analyst's forecasts with underlying business drivers and KPIs. They would also show how the data can enhance the accuracy and reliability of the estimates, providing tangible evidence of the data product's value.

PROVIDING POST-SALE SUPPORT:

Sales engineers continue to support clients after the sale, aiding with data integration, answering technical queries, and addressing any challenges that may arise.

Example: Post-sale, the sales engineer could work with the financial analyst to integrate the consumer spending data into their forecasting models and provide ongoing support in interpreting the data, identifying trends, and refining the models for better forecasting accuracy. This ongoing support is important for ensuring the long-term success and satisfaction of the client. By being a consistent presence and a reliable resource, the sales engineer builds trust and strengthens the relationship between the data provider and the client.

The Future of the DaaS Industry in an AI-Saturated Landscape

As the world becomes increasingly saturated with artificial intelligence (AI), the Data-as-a-Service (DaaS) industry finds itself at a critical juncture. The rapid advancement of AI technologies has led some to question the future relevance of curated data provision. After all, if AI models can directly consume raw data and extract meaningful insights, what role will DaaS companies play?

At first glance, it might seem that AI's raw computational might bypass traditional data services. As models become more sophisticated, they might appear to simply ingest vast oceans of raw data, distilling insights without the need for data curation, processing, or structuring. However, this view oversimplifies the complex relationship between AI and data. While AI models are indeed becoming more sophisticated and capable of processing vast amounts of raw data, they still heavily rely on high-quality, well-structured data to function effectively. Without the right data inputs, even the most advanced AI models will struggle to generate accurate and meaningful insights.

The reality is that raw data, no matter how extensive, is often noisy, inconsistent, and potentially misleading. To derive truly actionable insights, AI models require data that is contextually relevant, domain-specific, and carefully curated. This is where the future potential of the DaaS industry lies. Rather than directly competing with AI, DaaS companies have the opportunity to evolve and become indispensable partners in the AI ecosystem. By specializing in the intricate process of preparing and integrating data for AI consumption, DaaS companies can bridge the gap between raw data and AI-ready insights.

Imagine a new breed of DaaS companies—let's call them AI data integrators—that focus exclusively on the critical task of connecting data sets to complex AI models. These companies would leverage their deep understanding of both data and AI to ensure seamless compatibility and optimal performance.

AI data integrators would serve as the essential link between the vast universe of raw data and the increasingly sophisticated world of AI. They would be responsible for formatting, cleaning, and structuring data to meet the specific requirements of different AI models and applications. Doing so would enable organizations to fully harness the power of their data assets and allow AI companies to focus on building more advanced and specialized models.

The value proposition of AI data integrators would be multifaceted. They would help organizations navigate the complexities of data preparation and integration, ensuring that their data is AI-ready and optimized for maximum insight generation. They would also work closely with AI companies to understand their specific data requirements and develop customized data pipelines that feed directly into their models.

AI data integrators would play a crucial role in ensuring the quality, reliability, and ethical integrity of the data being fed into AI systems. As AI becomes more ubiquitous and influential in decision-making processes, the importance of unbiased, representative, and accurate data cannot be overstated. AI data integrators would be responsible for implementing rigorous data governance frameworks, conducting regular data audits, and ensuring compliance with relevant regulations and best practices.

The emergence of AI data integrators would not only benefit the DaaS industry but also the broader AI ecosystem. By providing a reliable and efficient conduit between raw data and AI models, these companies would accelerate the adoption and implementation of AI across various industries and use cases. They would help democratize AI by making it more accessible to organizations that may not have the in-house expertise or resources to handle the complexities of data preparation and integration.

Furthermore, the rise of AI data integrators would foster greater collaboration and innovation within the AI community. By working closely with AI developers and researchers, these companies would gain valuable insights into the latest trends, techniques, and best practices in AI. They would also be well-positioned to identify new opportunities for data-driven innovation and develop proprietary data sets and algorithms that could further enhance the capabilities of AI models.

The future of the DaaS industry in an AI-saturated landscape is not one of fierce competition but of evolution and specialization. By becoming AI data integrators, DaaS companies can carve out a vital niche in the AI ecosystem and play a critical role in unlocking the full potential of AI.

DATA-MINDED

As the demand for high-quality, AI-ready data continues to grow, the importance of these specialized DaaS companies will only increase. Those who can successfully navigate the complexities of data preparation and integration while maintaining a deep understanding of AI technologies will be well-positioned to thrive in the era of ubiquitous AI.

CONTEXTUAL MAPPING:

AI models, while increasingly sophisticated, require a clear understanding of data's contextual nuances. This is especially significant for domain-specific applications where data's meaning might vary based on external conditions or temporal relevance. DaaS companies can enhance their offerings by providing contextual data metadata—additional layers of information that help AI distinguish between, for example, financial data from different decades impacted by diverse economic factors. By evolving into contextual architects, DaaS firms ensure that AI models are always grounded in the right interpretive frame, optimizing the accuracy and relevance of insights they derive.

DATA HYGIENE AND COMPATIBILITY:

While AI possesses the computational might to sift through vast data arrays, the presence of inconsistencies, anomalies, or misalignments can compromise the quality of insights. DaaS companies can amplify their role by transitioning into data quality guarantors. By ensuring that the data is cleansed, standardized, and tailored for specific AI frameworks, these companies can ensure that AI doesn't only get a data deluge but receives a well-curated stream, positioning the models to generate sharper, more accurate insights.

ETHICAL AND RESPONSIBLE DATA FEEDING:

The challenge of data biases and their potential to inadvertently skew AI decisions is a critical concern. As stewards of ethical data consumption, DaaS companies can position themselves as bias auditors, ensuring that the datasets they provide have been examined for potential biases. By doing so, they help craft AI models that generate predictions and recommendations that are just and equitable and don't amplify societal disparities. For example, building HR systems to assist in selecting candidates for open roles.

FEEDBACK LOOPS:

The iterative nature of AI learning presents a dynamic opportunity for DaaS providers. By becoming feedback facilitators, these companies can actively participate in the AI learning process. They can channel feedback from AI systems back into their data curation processes, refining datasets based on AI learnings and ensuring the data is always optimized for the evolving needs of AI models.

MIDDLEWARE INTERFACE EXPERTISE AND LLM DATA PREPARATION:

The rise of advanced large language models, or LLMs, has showcased the importance of nuanced data feeding. DaaS companies can position themselves at the forefront of this evolution by becoming adept at molding and structuring data specifically for these language models. The task involves more than just feeding textual information; it's about understanding the syntactic, semantic, and contextual intricacies that LLMs thrive upon. This expertise can be pivotal in ensuring that AI systems generate responses or insights that are coherent, contextually aligned, and rich in substance. Moreover, as middleware interface experts, these companies can serve as a link between vast data reservoirs and the end AI applications, streamlining the data flow, ensuring real-time data updates, and optimizing model performance. By mastering this niche, DaaS firms can become indispensable in the chain of AI application development, reinforcing their value in an AI-driven ecosystem.

These AI data integrators would elevate the DaaS industry's value proposition. Instead of merely offering data, the industry would evolve to ensure that data is not only high-quality but also AI-ready, primed for maximum utility. This shift would require DaaS companies to develop new skills and capabilities, such as data annotation, data labeling, and data validation, to ensure their data offerings are optimized for AI consumption. By doing so, DaaS companies can differentiate themselves in an increasingly competitive market and provide greater value to their customers who are looking to leverage AI to drive business outcomes. This expansion of the DaaS industry would not only benefit the companies themselves but also accelerate the adoption and implementation of AI across various sectors, as organizations would have access to high-quality, AI-ready data that can be easily integrated into their existing systems and workflows.

As the AI revolution continues to surge across sectors, it isn't displacing the DaaS industry but expanding its horizons.

The intricate dance between data and AI is paving the way for an enriched DaaS ecosystem. This burgeoning landscape is set to encompass AI data integrators and specialized AI tailored to distinct data sets and verticals. Embracing this transformation, the DaaS industry is not just maintaining its relevance but is on the brink of a grander evolution in an AI-infused era. The future of the DaaS industry lies in its ability to adapt and innovate in response to the changing technological landscape, and those companies that can successfully navigate this transition will be well-positioned to thrive in the years to come. As AI continues to permeate every aspect of our lives and businesses, the role of DaaS companies as the critical link between data and AI will become paramount.

In Review:

- **Unique Nature of Data Sales:** We examined the unique challenges in selling data products, noting the difference from traditional software or service sales and the need to create a narrative around the untapped potential of data.

- **Crafting the Perfect Data Sample:** We discussed the art of creating data samples for prospective customers, balancing showcasing value without oversharing, and aligning the sample with customer needs while protecting intellectual property.

- **Understanding and Addressing Customer Needs:** We emphasized the importance of deeply understanding customer objectives and challenges in order to tailor data samples that demonstrate how the data can solve specific issues.

- **Balancing Transparency and Salesmanship in Data Sales:** We explored the delicate balance required in data sales between highlighting the data's strengths and maintaining ethical transparency about its capabilities and limitations.

- **Role of Sales Engineers in Data Sales:** We highlighted the critical role of sales engineers in the data sales process, who bridge the gap between the technical aspects of data products and the client's specific needs.

- **Misconceptions About Data Sales:** We addressed common misconceptions in data sales, contrasting the structured sales process in software with the more creative, solutions-oriented approach required in data sales.

- **Ethical and Responsible Data Representation:** We stressed the importance of ethical practices in data sales, including honesty and transparency, to maintain trust and reputation in the long run.

- **Navigating the Unique Dynamics of Data Sales:** We concluded with insights into the unique dynamics of data sales, emphasizing the necessity of understanding both the data being sold and the specific needs and context of the client for successful sales outcomes.

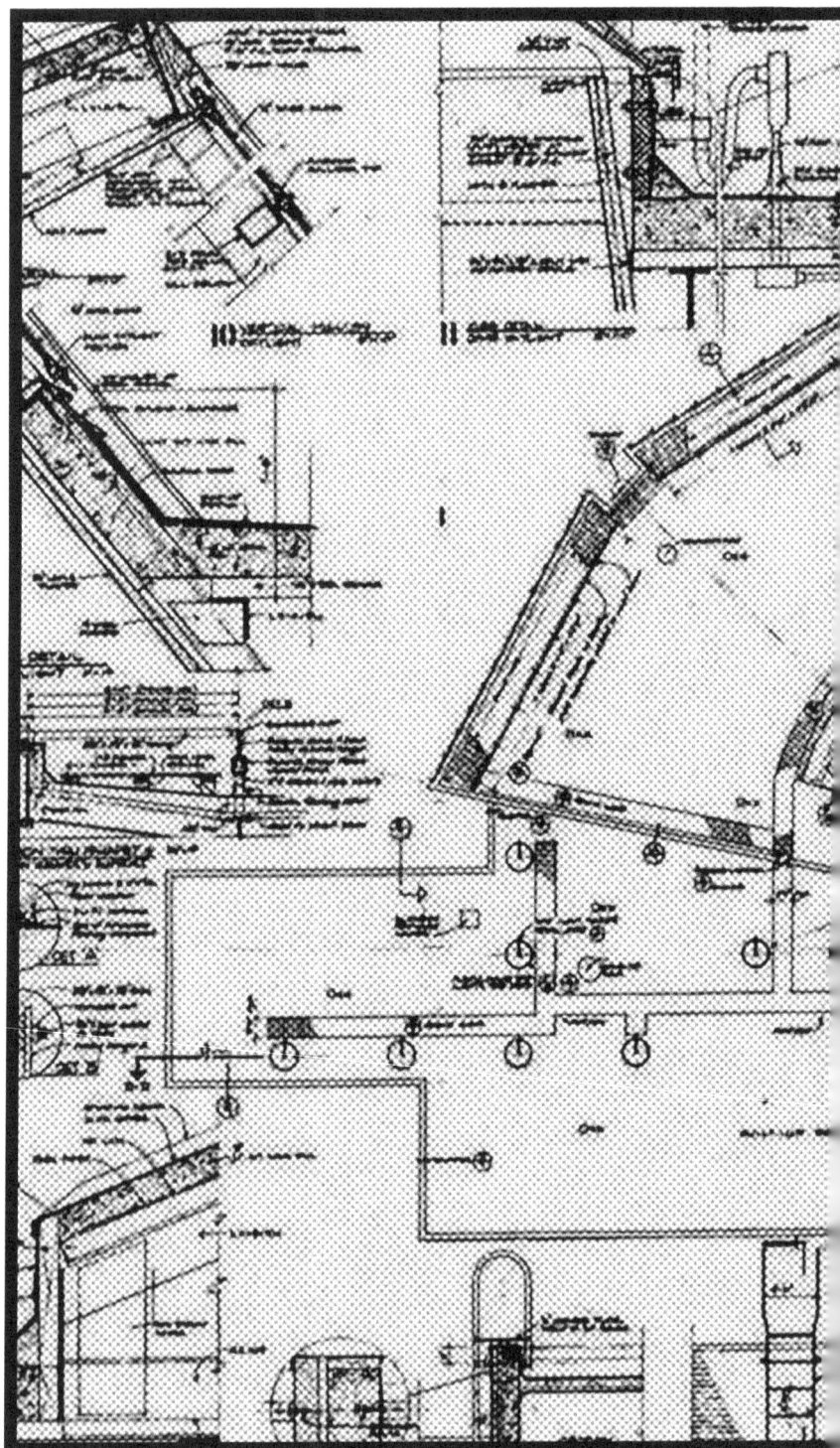

CHAPTER 5

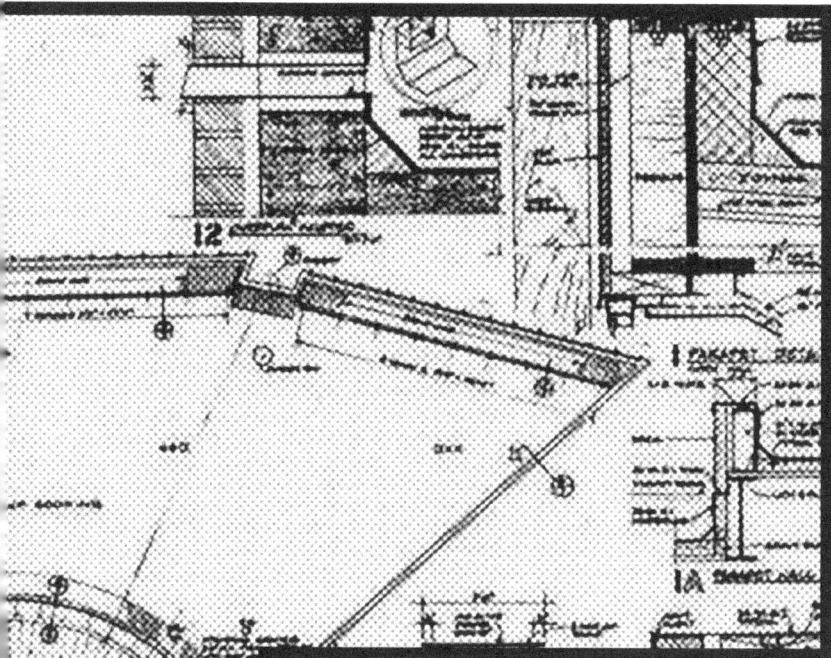

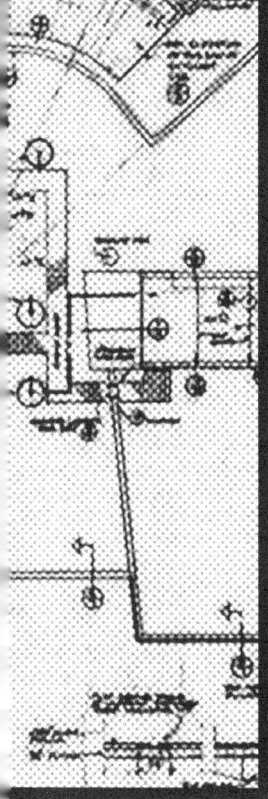

CRAFTING A COMPELLING
BUSINESS CASE

CRAFTING A COMPELLING BUSINESS CASE

The essence of a successful data business lies in a strong business case that provides the rationale for the venture, articulates the value proposition, and presents a persuasive argument for its viability and profitability. It serves as a roadmap, guiding your journey from concept to reality, and is the key to unlocking the support and resources needed to bring your vision to life. A compelling business case not only showcases the potential of your data business but also demonstrates your understanding of the market, your target audience, and the unique value you bring to the table. Crafting a strong business case requires a deep understanding of the data landscape, a keen sense of market dynamics, and the ability to articulate your data's value proposition.

In this chapter, we will cover intricacies to build a strong business case for a data business. Whether you are a startup founder, a data scientist with a vision, or a seasoned entrepreneur considering entering the data space, understanding the business dynamics is central to making informed decisions and establishing a sustainable and profitable data business. We'll cover four steps to crafting a compelling business case:

Defining the Business Model:

At the core of your data business is the business model. What is the framework that supports the value generation of your data business? How will you deliver value to your customers, and how will you capture value in return?

Identifying Your Market:

Knowing your audience is vital. Who are your potential customers? What problems are they looking to solve, and how does your data help solve those problems? Clearly defining your market and understanding its unique characteristics is essential for seizing the right opportunities.

Assessing Data Value:

Not all data is of equal value. How do you determine the value of your data? What makes your data unique, and why would customers be willing to pay for it?

Understanding and Leveraging Your Unfair Advantage:

What sets you apart in a competitive marketplace? Do you have unique access to data or a novel approach to data analysis? Navigating through a vast network of potential customers can be daunting. However, by pinpointing and leveraging your unique strengths, you can refine your value proposition and set your data business apart from the competition. This process involves not only recognizing your unfair advantage but also strategically aligning it with the needs and preferences of your target market. By focusing on customers who resonate with your distinct offerings, you can cultivate stronger relationships and position your business for sustained success in the competitive marketplace.

We will tackle each of these components in detail, exploring how to create a robust business case that resonates with potential investors, customers, and stakeholders.

Defining a Business Model

The foundation of a successful data business lies in its business model. A well-defined business model serves as a blueprint, outlining how the organization will create, deliver, and capture value in the market. It encompasses the key components of the business, including the value proposition, target customer segments, revenue streams, cost structure, and critical resources and activities.

In the context of a data business, the business model revolves around the collection, processing, analysis, and monetization of data. It defines how the business will transform raw data into valuable insights and solutions that address the needs of its target customers. The choice of business model is crucial, as it directly impacts the data business's sustainability, scalability, and profitability.

There are several common business models that data businesses can adopt, each with its own advantages and challenges. Let's explore five prominent business models in more detail:

DATA-AS-A-SERVICE (DAAS):

The Data-as-a-Service model is a cloud-based approach to delivering data to customers on demand. In this model, the data provider hosts and manages large datasets on their own cloud infrastructure, making it easily accessible to customers via APIs or web-based interfaces. Customers pay a recurring subscription fee to access the data, which they can then integrate into their own applications, analytics platforms, or business processes.

One key advantage of the DaaS model is its scalability. As the data provider manages the infrastructure, they can easily accommodate growing demand by allocating more resources to their cloud platform. This allows customers to access the data they need without worrying about storage, processing, or maintenance.

Another benefit of DaaS is the predictability of revenue streams for the data provider. With customers paying a recurring subscription fee, the data business can forecast its revenue more accurately and plan its growth strategies accordingly.

Quandl: Provides financial, economic, and alternative data on a subscription basis to investment professionals.

Google Maps: Offers APIs for maps, geolocation, and other geospatial services, which businesses can subscribe to and integrate into their own applications.

DATA LICENSING:

In the data licensing model, the data provider grants customers the right to use a specific dataset for a defined period, typically in exchange for a one-time or recurring fee. The data provider retains ownership of the data and controls how it can be used, distributed, and modified by the licensee.

Data licensing is often used for specialized or proprietary datasets with high value for specific industries or use cases. For example, a company that collects and curates data on consumer behavior might license its dataset to marketing agencies or retail businesses to help them make better decisions around product development, pricing, and advertising.

One advantage of data licensing is that it can provide upfront revenue for the data business, as customers often pay a significant fee to access the data. Additionally, data licensing allows the provider to maintain control over their data assets and prevent unauthorized use or distribution.

However, data licensing also has some limitations. Since the data is typically provided as a static snapshot, customers may need to purchase updates or new licenses to access the most current data. Moreover, the licensing terms may restrict how the data can be used, shared, or integrated with other datasets, which can limit its utility for some customers.

Nielsen: Licenses its media and consumer data to brands, advertising agencies, and media companies.

Acxiom: Licenses its consumer data for marketing, risk mitigation, and people-based marketing initiatives.

DATA BROKERAGE:

Data brokers are companies that specialize in collecting, aggregating, and selling data from various sources to businesses or other organizations. They act as intermediaries between data providers and data consumers, helping to facilitate data exchange for various purposes, such as marketing, risk assessment, or research.

Data brokers typically collect data from a wide range of public and private sources, including government records, social media, web browsing behavior, and commercial transactions. They then clean, process, and enrich the data to make it more valuable and actionable for their customers.

One of the key advantages of the data brokerage model is that it allows businesses to access a wide range of data without having to collect or manage it themselves. This can be particularly useful for small or mid-sized companies that may not have the resources or expertise to gather and process large volumes of data on their own.

However, data brokerage also raises concerns around privacy and security, as individuals may not be aware that their personal data is being collected and sold by these companies. As a result, data brokers are subject to increasing regulation and scrutiny, particularly in jurisdictions like the European Union, where the General Data Protection Regulation (GDPR) imposes strict rules around collecting and using personal data.

Equifax, Experian, and TransUnion: The three major credit reporting agencies collect and sell consumer credit data to lenders, insurers, and other businesses.

LiveRamp: Provides identity resolution services to connect customer data across multiple platforms for better targeting and measurement.

DATA ANALYSIS AND INSIGHTS:

In the data analysis and insights model, the data business goes beyond simply providing access to raw data. It offers value-added services in the form of advanced analytics, insights, and recommendations. This model recognizes that many organizations may not have the in-house expertise or resources to analyze large and complex datasets on their own and, therefore, require the assistance (or a product) of specialized data analytics providers.

Data analysis and insights providers typically offer a range of services, including data mining, predictive modeling, machine learning, and data visualization. They work closely with their customers to understand their specific business needs and challenges and then use their expertise and tools to extract meaningful insights and actionable intelligence from the data.

A key benefit of this model is that it allows businesses to leverage the expertise of specialized data analysts and data scientists without having to hire them in-house. This can be particularly valuable for organizations that have limited resources or that require insights on a project-by-project basis.

Moreover, by offering a higher-value service beyond raw data access, data analysis and insights providers can often charge premium prices for their services, leading to higher profit margins than other data business models.

Palantir: Offers data analysis platforms that help organizations integrate, analyze, and visualize large datasets to derive actionable insights.

Numerator: Provides omnichannel market intelligence and insights using proprietary data collected from its extensive panel of consumers.

FREEMIUM MODEL:

The freemium model pricing strategy has become increasingly popular among data businesses in recent years. Under this model, the data provider offers a free basic version of their product or service, with the option for customers to upgrade to a paid premium version that includes additional features, functionalities, or data access.

The rationale behind the freemium model is that by offering a free version of the product, the data business can attract a large volume of users and build brand awareness, expecting that a certain percentage of these users will eventually convert to paying customers.

The free version of the product typically has limited functionality or data access, designed to give users a taste of the value that the product can provide. The premium version, on the other hand, includes advanced features, larger data volumes, or more granular data that is valuable for users who require more sophisticated analysis or insights.

One advantage of the freemium model is that it allows data businesses to build a large user base quickly and at a relatively low cost. By offering a free version of the data product, the data provider can lower the barriers to adoption and encourage more users to try out their service.

However, the freemium model also has some challenges. For example, the data business needs to strike the right balance between offering enough value in the free version to attract users while still holding back enough features or data to incentivize upgrades to the paid version. Moreover, the data provider needs to have a clear understanding of their customer acquisition costs and lifetime value to ensure that they can generate enough revenue from their paid users to offset the costs of supporting their free users.

Kaggle: Offers free access to a wide range of datasets and machine learning competitions. Users can upgrade to Kaggle Pro for additional features and benefits.

FRED (Federal Reserve Economic Data): Provides free access to a large dataset of economic and financial data. Premium services and data products are available for a fee.

Each of these business models has its advantages and drawbacks. Selecting the right business model requires careful consideration of factors such as the nature of the data, the target market, the competitive landscape, and the resources available to the business. It is essential to test and validate the chosen business model, continuously monitor its performance, and be willing to adapt and pivot as market conditions and customer needs evolve.

Throughout this chapter, we'll refer to each business model, provide examples, and offer guidance on how to choose and implement the most suitable model for your data business.

Misconceptions: Linear vs. Critical Mass Financing

The financing and fundraising dynamics for software and data companies are starkly different, primarily due to the contrasting paths of value creation in these business models. This is due to the fundamental differences in how value is created and realized in these two types of businesses.

A typical software company's value creation process tends to be linear and incremental. A small team of engineers can start building a minimum viable product (MVP) with relatively humble resources and then gradually enhance and expand the software over time as they receive feedback from users and attract more funding. Each new feature, bug fix, or performance improvement adds incremental value to the software, making it more attractive and valuable to users and investors alike.

This linear value creation process enables software companies to start small and scale up gradually, following a relatively predictable financing trajectory. They can raise smaller rounds of funding at the beginning to get the product off the ground and then pursue larger investments as they demonstrate traction and market potential. This allows software companies to minimize dilution for founders and early investors while providing a clear path to growth and profitability.

In contrast, data companies often face a much more challenging financing landscape due to the nature of their value-creation process. Unlike software, which can be built and delivered incrementally, data products typically require a significant upfront investment in data acquisition, processing, and refinement before they can provide meaningful value to customers.

This is because the value of a data product is largely determined by the quality, depth, and breadth of the underlying data assets. A small or incomplete dataset is often of little use to customers, as it cannot support robust analytics or provide comprehensive insights. To be truly valuable, a data product must achieve a certain 'critical mass' of high-quality, relevant data covering a wide range of use cases and customer needs.

Reaching this critical mass often requires data companies to invest heavily in data collection, cleaning, integration, and enrichment long before they can start monetizing their data products. This upfront investment can be substantial, often running into the millions or even tens of millions of dollars, depending on the scope and complexity of the data being collected.

Moreover, the time horizon for realizing a return on this investment can be much longer than for software products. While a software MVP can start generating revenue almost immediately, a data product may need months or even years of data accumulation and refinement before it can start delivering value to customers. This extended 'gestation period' can be challenging for data companies and their investors, as it requires significant patience and a long-term vision for the business.

Given these challenges, data companies often need to approach financing and fundraising in a very different way than software companies. Instead of relying on a linear, incremental funding model, they may need to raise more significant amounts of capital upfront to finance the data acquisition and refinement process. This can involve seeking out strategic investors who have a deep understanding of the data market and are willing to take a long-term view of the business.

Data companies may also need to focus more on building a powerful narrative around the future value of their data assets rather than emphasizing short-term revenue or user growth metrics. This narrative needs to articulate the unique capabilities of the data being collected, the large and growing market opportunity it addresses, and the competitive advantages that the company has in acquiring and refining this data over time.

Ultimately, the key to successful financing for data companies is to find investors who share the company's long-term vision and are willing to back that vision with patient capital. This requires a different mindset and approach than traditional software investing, which tends to focus more on short-term metrics and quick exits.

By understanding these fundamental differences between linear and critical mass financing, data entrepreneurs can develop more effective fundraising strategies and build stronger partnerships with investors who are aligned with their long-term goals. While the path to success may be longer and more challenging for data companies, the potential rewards are also much greater, as those who are able to achieve critical mass and build truly valuable data assets will be well-positioned to dominate their markets for years to come.

Identifying Your Market

Successfully navigating the data business landscape begins with a clear understanding of your target market. Identifying who needs your data, why they need it, and how they intend to use it are fundamental questions that must be answered. This process is akin to establishing the product-market fit in traditional businesses but adapted for the data business landscape. Let's discuss six key components of defining your market in the context of a data business.

MARKET SIZE AND POTENTIAL:

Understanding the size of your target market is fundamental. You need to evaluate the number of potential customers, their willingness to pay, and the potential revenue you could generate.

Example: If you're targeting small e-commerce businesses, you may have many potential customers but a lower price point. Conversely, if you're targeting large corporations, you may have fewer potential customers but a higher price point.

CUSTOMER NEEDS AND PAIN POINTS:

Understanding customer needs and pain points allows data companies to tailor their offerings to address specific challenges. Do your customers struggle with understanding their target audience? Do they need help with forecasting sales? What jobs are they trying to hire your data for?

Example: If your target market is e-commerce businesses looking to optimize their advertising campaigns, you could offer them insights into consumer behavior and purchasing trends.

DATA AVAILABILITY AND UNIQUENESS:

Consider whether the data you are offering is readily available elsewhere and what makes your data unique. Are you offering a novel dataset that can't be found anywhere else? Or are you providing a unique analysis that adds value to existing data? Understanding what sets your data apart will help you position it more effectively.

Example: If your target market is healthcare organizations looking for patient data, offering a unique dataset that includes detailed patient demographics, medical history, and treatment outcomes could make your data more valuable.

MARKET TRENDS AND CHANGES:

Keeping up to date with market trends and changes is essential. Are there shifts in the industry that might affect your target market? Are there new technologies or regulations that could impact data usage? By staying current with these changes, you can adjust your offerings to meet your customers' evolving needs.

Example: If your target market is financial institutions and there is a new regulation that affects data privacy, you could offer them insights into how to navigate this new landscape and comply with the new rules.

COMPETITIVE LANDSCAPE:

What data are your competitors offering? How do they package and price their data? Knowing this information will help you differentiate your data products and identify areas where you can add value.

Example: If your target market is retail businesses, and your competitors are offering standard sales data, you could differentiate yourself by providing more granular data that includes customer demographics, purchasing habits, and loyalty program data.

UNDERSTANDING DATA CONSUMPTION PATTERNS:

It's vital to recognize how your target market typically consumes data. Do they have large data science teams that can handle raw data and perform their own analysis? Are they more accustomed to dashboards and visualizations? Understanding these patterns will help you tailor your data offerings to fit their needs and enhance the user experience.

Incorporating these considerations into your market definition will help you create a more comprehensive and actionable understanding of your target market. This deep understanding will serve as a solid foundation for your data business and help you effectively connect with your audience.

Assessing Value: More Than Just Numbers

Unlike tangible products or traditional services, data does not have a universally accepted price tag or value metric. Instead, its value is largely subjective and varies depending on the specific needs and use cases of your target market.

Assessing the value of your data is an important step in building a robust business case for your data offerings. In addition to volume or data points, your assessment should consider eight key factors: relevance, accuracy, granularity, timeliness, exclusivity, compliance, usability, and scalability. Each of these aspects plays a key role in shaping the perceived value of your data and, ultimately, in driving your data business's success.

Here, we'll discuss these factors in detail and provide actionable insights to help you assess and enhance the value of your data for your target market. Through a holistic and comprehensive approach to assessing value, you can better position your data business for success and create data offerings that resonate with your customers' needs and preferences.

RELEVANCE:

Data relevance involves addressing the specific needs of your target audience. Suppose you are offering transaction data to retailers. If you provide transaction data that focuses on a particular age group that aligns with your target retailer's audience, such as millennial purchasing habits, your data becomes highly relevant. Similarly, consider the geographic relevance of your data. Does your data capture the behavior of consumers in a particular region that interests your customers? You must either shape your target customers to the ground truth of your data, or you need to improve your data until it will be relevant to your ideal customer.

ACCURACY:

High-quality data is critical to the decision-making process. Your data sources should be reliable and trustworthy. If you're offering satellite imagery to agricultural businesses, ensure that your images come from trusted sources, such as high-resolution satellite providers, and that they're processed with precision to avoid errors in interpretation. Validate your data against reputable sources to ensure accuracy. For example, if you're offering consumer spending data, verify it with US Bureau of Economics expenditure records.

GRANULARITY:

Granular data provides detailed insights that can be critical for strategic decision-making. Suppose you're providing social media sentiment data to brands. If your data can break down sentiments by demographics, such as age, gender, or location, brands can tailor their marketing campaigns to target specific groups. For instance, if your data shows that younger people respond more positively to eco-friendly campaigns, brands can use this insight to craft targeted messages.

TIMELINESS:

Updated data is important for decision-making in rapidly changing environments. If you're offering stock market data, providing real-time data helps traders make timely decisions. In sectors where data changes rapidly, such as financial markets, weather, or news, it's vital to offer data that is updated at least daily or in real-time to ensure your clients have access to the latest trends and can respond quickly.

EXCLUSIVITY:

Exclusive data can set you apart from competitors and justify premium pricing. If you're offering proprietary research data, what makes your data unique? Is it access to a particular dataset, expertise in a specific field, or a proprietary algorithm that provides insights unavailable elsewhere? For example, a company with unique access to specific satellite data could offer insights into crop health that are unavailable to others.

COMPLIANCE:

Ensuring data compliance adds value to your data by making it safer and more trustworthy. Compliance could involve de-identifying personal information, ensuring data collection methods are transparent and meet regulatory standards, or having robust data security protocols. For example, if you're offering consumer data and don't need to be able to identify individuals, create cohorts of users that align with the use cases you're building for (e.g., by geographies or behaviors). Ensuring that information is collected with explicit consent can add value to your data.

USABILITY:

Easily usable data is essential for businesses with limited resources or technical expertise. Make your data easy to integrate with commonly used tools or platforms. This means providing APIs, offering data in standard formats, or providing tools to help clients work with your data. For example, if you're offering web traffic data, structuring it in a way that can be easily imported into standard analytics tools can add value.

SCALABILITY:

Scalable data solutions that can be adjusted according to customer needs add versatility to your offerings. By providing data packages tailored to businesses of different sizes, you can appeal to a wider range of customers. For example, if you're offering sales data, you could have different pricing and data volume options for startups, mid-sized companies, and large corporations, allowing each to access the data they need at a price they can afford.

Understanding Your Unfair Advantage

Building a successful data business is not just about having access to vast amounts of data or a unique dataset; it's about identifying and leveraging your unfair advantage. Your unfair advantage is the unique aspect or combination of factors that sets you apart from competitors and creates a defensible position in the market.

Your unfair advantage could be derived from various sources, such as access to exclusive data, proprietary technology, strong relationships with key customers, or deep domain expertise. Understanding and capitalizing on your unfair advantage is indispensable for building a sustainable and profitable data business.

Let's explore five different types of unfair advantages and provide guidance on how to identify and leverage your own unfair advantage in the data industry.

EXCLUSIVE DATA

Access to a unique or exclusive data source can be a strong unfair advantage. This could be the result of an exclusive partnership, proprietary data collection methods, or a unique perspective on existing data.

Example: Experian is a well-known credit reporting agency with access to credit-related data on millions of consumers. Due to its unique position as a credit bureau, it has exclusive access to certain types of data that its competitors do not.

TECHNOLOGICAL EDGE

Possessing proprietary technology, advanced analytics, or AI capabilities often serves as a key differentiator in the data business. If you can process, analyze, or present data more efficiently or effectively than competitors, it's a significant advantage.

Example: Palantir has developed proprietary software platforms that enable organizations to integrate, manage, and analyze large datasets. Its technology gives it a competitive edge in serving clients with complex data needs.

STRONG CUSTOMER RELATIONSHIPS

Deep relationships with key customers can provide an edge in the data business. Long-standing trust and familiarity with customer needs can enable you to tailor your data offerings more effectively.

Example: Nielsen has long-standing relationships with major television networks and advertisers. These relationships allow Nielsen to understand their specific needs and offer data products that are tailored to their industry.

UNIQUE DOMAIN EXPERTISE

Expertise in a specific industry or domain can give you a leg up in the data business. This knowledge can enable you to better understand and meet the unique data needs of a particular sector.

Example: Orbital Insight is a company that leverages geospatial data and artificial intelligence to provide insights into economic trends. They specialize in analyzing satellite and drone images to extract valuable information for various industries such as retail, agriculture, and finance. Their deep expertise in interpreting these images allows them to offer data products that give their clients unique perspectives on crop yields, supply chain disruptions, retail store traffic, etc.

DATA COMBINATIONS

The ability to integrate and analyze data from multiple sources to create new, valuable insights can set you apart from competitors. Combining data sources can yield insights that are more valuable than the sum of their parts.

Example: Waze combines GPS data, user-submitted reports, and other data sources to provide real-time traffic updates and route recommendations. By integrating these diverse data sources, Waze offers unique insights to its users.

These factors can serve as a unique advantage in the data business. Identifying and leveraging your own unfair advantage is an important step for establishing a strong position in the market and building a sustainable and profitable data business.

AI's Seismic Impact on the Business Models of Data Companies

As we stand on the cusp of a new era, we all must recognize that the entwining of Artificial Intelligence (AI) and Data-as-a-Service (DaaS) isn't just a fleeting trend; it's the future of our industry. We're at the threshold of an era where the intertwining of AI and DaaS will exponentially amplify the value proposition for both sectors. This isn't just about modest, incremental changes. It's a seismic, qualitative leap that disrupts current paradigms and opens unforeseen opportunities. This section will explore speculative scenarios of AI shaping the future of DaaS, from emerging market opportunities to radical alterations in how businesses and individuals derive value from data.

The terrain is shifting, and those prepared to adapt will thrive in this new world of limitless opportunity, where leveraging AI is not just advisable but essential for building a compelling business model in the data industry. These two groundbreaking technologies both augment the existing data services landscape and also fundamentally alter our relationship with data itself by providing a consistent, scalable, and highly accessible interface to work with data and drive decisions. This is a future where AI, as Harvard Business School professor Karim Lakhani succinctly put it, "lowers the cost of cognition," thus democratizing data like never before.

Our optimism is fueled by the symbiotic relationship between AI and DaaS—a bond that holds the promise of mutual enrichment. With its capacity to process and analyze vast amounts of data, AI will inevitably expand the DaaS market by making data more accessible to the general public. It is gradually bridging the technological skill gap, empowering everyone from business leaders to junior staff to become data-literate and informed decision-makers.

Meanwhile, DaaS will be instrumental in the maturation and differentiation of AI technologies. The AI models of tomorrow will be uniquely potent if trained on specialized, proprietary data from DaaS providers. This reciprocal growth dynamic will enable AI technologies to offer unparalleled, data-backed solutions that set them apart in a crowded marketplace.

AI is more than a fad; it is the future. Let's discuss two ways to leverage AI and data into your business model.

LEVERAGING AI AND PUBLIC DATASETS

Much like businesses that were early adopters of the internet and online payments, organizations willing to adopt AI into their data processes will reap the rewards. One such way to do so early in an organization's development is the integration of public datasets. While the focus often lands on exclusive, proprietary data, let's not underestimate the transformative power of publicly available data. Until now, the fragmentation and complexity of these public data repositories, such as government statistics, have been a roadblock. But as AI technologies mature, they unlock new capabilities for DaaS companies to serve as the ultimate aggregators and integrators of this vast ocean of public information.

Imagine a future where DaaS companies act as the architects who build the vital conduits between these scattered but invaluable datasets and the AI engines that are optimized to process them. By consolidating and standardizing this dispersed data, DaaS firms can offer AI companies a single point of entry to a world of previously hard-to-access insights. In this hypothetical future, advances in AI will enable DaaS companies to efficiently categorize and serve this information in a manner that is highly usable for AI applications.

Take, for instance, AI models designed to reshape public policy or redefine urban planning. With streamlined access to harmonized, multifaceted data, these models could provide revolutionary insights. This isn't restricted to government data alone—envision DaaS companies tapping into diverse domains of public data, from academic research to global health statistics, and providing an invaluable resource for AI-driven innovation.

By seizing this opportunity, DaaS companies would be doing more than facilitating easier data access; they'd be democratizing the AI industry. Smaller AI enterprises, which may not have the resources to build extensive data pipelines, could compete based on their algorithms' strength and not just their data-gathering capabilities. This future—where DaaS companies can expand their offerings in ways previously thought too challenging, thanks to AI—promises a cascade of collaborative benefits that could elevate both industries to new heights of innovation and value.

LEVERAGING AI AND NON-PUBLIC DATASETS

The vast universe of data isn't confined to the public domain. Indeed, a considerable chunk of the most valuable and insightful data remains non-public, often held closely due to its sensitive or proprietary nature. As we stare into the future of AI's next transformation, the integration of high-quality, non-public datasets is poised to herald a significant evolution in generative AI. These datasets, rich in both depth and unique insights, provide the platform upon which generative AI can achieve newfound heights in both innovation and usability.

Consider the realm of legal practice, a discipline anchored by centuries of case law, legislation, and intricate legal reasoning. Today's large language models, or LLMs, have already demonstrated their prowess in understanding and generating legal language. However, imagine an LLM further fine-tuned on a curated dataset comprising not just publicly available case law but also non-public legal briefs from settlement cases, internal memos, and strategic legal communications. This enriched training would empower the LLM to become hyper-specialized in specific legal domains. Paired with such an AI, an attorney could derive insights from nuanced past cases, including those settled out of public view, ensuring a holistic understanding of potential legal outcomes. The AI's recommendations might encompass strategies gleaned from both successful and unsuccessful settlement cases, becoming an invaluable tool in legal strategizing.

Similarly, the medical field offers another potent example. Emergency rooms across the globe face the daily challenge of efficiently triaging incoming patients, determining the severity of their ailments, and prioritizing care. Now, consider an AI trained on a database filled with real patient data, symptoms, treatments, outcomes, and the intricacies of emergency room scenarios, including non-public data from past treatments and outcomes. Such an AI could rapidly analyze a patient's symptoms, cross-reference them with historical data, and suggest an immediate course of action. In doing so, it would streamline the ER process and play a pivotal role in improving patient outcomes by ensuring crucial medical interventions are timely.

There are countless examples, yet the consistent underlying theme is clear: integrating high-quality, non-public data into generative AI has the potential to profoundly alter the landscape. As we seek to further unlock the potential of AI, these non-public datasets become the lighthouse, guiding us towards applications previously thought to be in the realm of science fiction. The future is beckoning, and it's a future where generative AI, bolstered by these invaluable data treasures, reshapes industries and redefines what's possible.

In Review:

- **Defining the Business Model:** We explored the foundation of a data business, focusing on how it creates and delivers value, revenue streams, customer segments, cost structures, and other key elements.

- **Identifying the Market:** We stressed the importance of understanding the target audience, including their problems and how the data can solve them. We also emphasized the necessity of defining the market and understanding its unique characteristics.

- **Assessing Data Value:** We investigated how to determine the value of data by discussing factors like uniqueness, relevance to customers, and reasons that make data valuable and marketable.

- **Leveraging Unfair Advantage:** We examined the concept of an unfair advantage, such as unique data access or novel data analysis methods, which can be key to differentiating a data business in the market.

- **Business Models in Data Businesses:** We reviewed different business models, such as Data-as-a-Service (DaaS), Data Licensing, and Data Brokerage, and discussed their benefits and challenges.

- **Integrating AI with Data Business:** We discussed the potential for AI to enhance data services and the evolving role of AI in shaping data businesses, including the integration and application of AI technologies in DaaS.

- **Fundraising and Financing Challenges:** We addressed the unique challenges of financing a data business, highlighting the difference in value creation and the need for substantial upfront investment to reach critical mass.

- **Future Outlook for Data Businesses:** We concluded with insights into the future of data businesses, considering the evolving landscapes of AI, data regulations, market demands, and the necessity for data businesses to adapt and innovate continuously.

CONCLUSION
A NEW DAWN

A NEW DAWN

Our journey through the dynamic landscape of data businesses has been a source of inspiration. We have traversed from ancient times to the present day, witnessing how data collection has shaped our world. From the days of Mesopotamia and Egypt to the Renaissance and Industrial Revolution, and now to the vast opportunities and challenges unfolding today, the evolution of data collection and management has been nothing short of transformative. Writing, the printing press, and now the internet have all made it easier for everyone to access information and make our businesses data-driven at their core. This evolution has not only revolutionized how we do business but also had a profound impact on society, sparking optimism for a future driven by data.

Raw data, once confined to hand-written documents and storage warehouses, has undergone a remarkable transformation. It is now being converted into valuable insights and actionable intelligence across industries. Organizations have learned to harness advanced analytics, machine learning algorithms, and predictive modeling techniques to extract meaningful patterns and trends from vast troves of data, empowering decision-makers to make informed choices and drive business growth. The process of data productization was not merely about packaging data into consumable formats but about imbuing it with meaning and relevance—the transformation from a passive resource into a strategic asset.

As we dove into the challenges and opportunities of data businesses in the digital age, we also zoomed in on the ethical side of things, such as data privacy and security. With data becoming more of a commodity, there are greater worries about how personal information is used. Remember the Cambridge Analytica, mess or the Equifax breach? These major scandals showed why we need solid rules and guidelines to keep people's data safe and hold companies accountable. It is vital for organizations to scale up security with encryption, access controls, and regular check-ups to keep sensitive information secure and earn trust from customers and stakeholders. We must approach data privacy and security not merely as a legal or technical issue but as a fundamental pillar in the data industry. As data becomes increasingly central to our lives, we must ensure that individuals have control over their personal information and that their privacy is protected.

Moreover, we explored the intricacies of marketing and selling data products in a competitive marketplace. Unlike physical goods, data products are intangible, which means marketing and sales require a different approach. Companies must show customers why their data products matter, how they solve problems, and what results they bring. This might involve sharing thought-provoking content, real-life examples, and interactive demos to highlight what the data products can do. Businesses need to focus on building strong sales channels and nurturing relationships with important players to boost adoption and revenue. The key to success in marketing and selling data products is to focus on the underlying value they provide to customers and to communicate that value in a clear and enticing way. This requires a deep understanding of customer needs and a willingness to adapt and evolve in response to changing market conditions.

At the forefront of our examination is the pivotal emergence of Data-as-a-Service (DaaS) as a transformative powerhouse in the data realm. DaaS signifies a profound shift in how data is accessed, analyzed, and utilized, presenting organizations with unparalleled access to an extensive array of data-centric services and solutions. From harnessing cloud-based analytics platforms to accessing data on demand from specialized marketplaces, DaaS empowers organizations to swiftly access and utilize data in real-time, facilitating expedited decision-making and enhanced adaptability, all in response to evolving market dynamics. The rise of DaaS has not only transformed the way businesses operate but has also created new opportunities for innovation and growth. As more and more organizations adopt DaaS solutions, we can expect to see a wave of new applications and use cases emerge, driving forward the data transformation of industries and society as a whole.

By democratizing access to data, DaaS has the potential to level the playing field and empower organizations of all sizes to compete and innovate.

Yet, despite its potential, DaaS comes with its fair share of hurdles and obligations. As stewards of this digital landscape, organizations must confront ethical dilemmas concerning data privacy, security, and ownership. From regulations like GDPR in Europe to laws like CCPA in the US, governments worldwide are stepping in to safeguard individuals' rights and ensure companies are responsible for their data handling. It is important for organizations to prioritize observing these rules and embracing ethical data practices to foster trust among customers and stakeholders.

The future of data businesses is filled with both excitement and uncertainty. The potential of DaaS to drive innovation, foster collaboration, and address pressing societal challenges is immense. From personalized healthcare and education to smart cities and sustainable development, the applications of DaaS are as diverse as they are impactful. However, realizing this potential will require concerted efforts from all stakeholders—from policymakers and industry leaders to consumers and ordinary citizens—to ensure that the benefits of DaaS are realized equitably and sustainably.

As we have journeyed through the data business landscape, it's clear that data has immense power to shape our future. From ancient times to the present, its story is about change, creativity, and endless potential. For those eager to dive into the world of data businesses, here's the deal: we're on the cusp of a new era driven by data. It's time to tackle the challenges and seize the opportunities ahead. But remember, it's not just about innovation—it's about doing it right.

Welcome to the new frontier of data!

.

INDEX

DATA-MINDED